# ACTIVITIES LINKING

# SCIENCE

## WITH

# MATH

# 5-8

# ACTIVITIES
# LINKING
# SCIENCE
## WITH
# MATH
# 5-8

**John Eichinger**

NSTApress
National Science Teachers Association

National Science Teachers Association

Claire Reinburg, Director
Jennifer Horak, Managing Editor
Judy Cusick, Senior Editor
Andrew Cocke, Associate Editor

ART AND DESIGN
Will Thomas Jr., Director
Joseph Butera, Graphic Designer, cover and interior design

PRINTING AND PRODUCTION
Catherine Lorrain, Director

NATIONAL SCIENCE TEACHERS ASSOCIATION
Francis Q. Eberle, PhD, Executive Director
David Beacom, Publisher

Copyright © 2009 by the National Science Teachers Association.
All rights reserved. Printed in the United States of America.
12 11 10 09    4 3 2 1
This book was previously published by Pearson Education, Inc.

LIBRARY OF CONGRESS CATALOGING-IN-PUBLICATION DATA
Eichinger, John.
  Activities linking science with mathematics, grades K-4 / by John Eichinger.
     p. cm.
  Includes bibliographical references and index.
  ISBN 978-1-933531-42-7
  1. Science--Study and teaching (Elementary)--Activity programs. 2. Mathematics--Study and
teaching (Elementary)--Activity programs. 3. Interdisciplinary approach in education. I. Title.
  LB1585.E36 2009
  372.3'5044--dc22
                        2009003257

# Table of Contents

# Earth Science

# Life Science

# Acknowledgments

I would like to thank NSTA Press for supporting this probe into integrated science instruction and am particularly indebted to Claire Reinburg and Jennifer Horak for their clear vision and expert guidance. I am grateful to the reviewers for sharing their excellent comments and insights, and offer special thanks to my education students at California State University, Los Angeles, who continue to enlighten and inspire me. Thanks also to my colleagues Chogollah Maroufi, Paul Narguizian, and Gregory Toliver for their generous encouragement and feedback. I am especially grateful to my wife, Danube, and my sons, Wolfe and Björn, for their unwavering patience and boundless support, without which this book would not exist.

**John Eichinger**

*Lovingly dedicated to Danube, Wolfe, and Björn*

# + Introduction

*"The solution which I am urging, is to eradicate the fatal disconnection of subjects which kills the vitality of our modern curriculum. There is only one subject matter for education, and that is Life in all its manifestations."*

**Alfred North Whitehead**
*(The Aims of Education 1929)*

*Activities Linking Science With Mathematics, Grades 5–8 (ALSM)* rejects traditional, discipline-bound methods of instruction and instead opens the door to hands-on, discovery-based, and academically rigorous activities that link various scientific disciplines to mathematics in particular, but also to visual arts, social sciences, and language arts. These 20 activities, intended for inservice and preservice teachers in grades 5–8, align with the National Science Education Standards (NSES) and the National Council of Teachers of Mathematics (NCTM) standards, both of which encourage an increase in interdisciplinary instruction. The activities balance integrated content with the processes of personally relevant inquiry and are designed to promote creative, critical thinking on the part of all students. The activities are also teacher friendly; they require no advanced expertise in any particular subject area, and they use inexpensive and easy-to-find materials.

*ALSM* is an engaging supplement to core classroom curriculum that allows all teachers to maintain high expectations with effective, authentic, and student-centered instruction. Preservice teachers, in particular, benefit from an early introduction to these sorts of strategies, helping them develop effective interdisciplinary classroom instruction. Indeed, as McComas and Wang noted, teachers must "experience effective blended science instruction models firsthand" for true interdisciplinary models ever to flourish in our education system (1998, p. 345). To that end, this book models alternative, yet proven, teaching practices that can be applied in any grade 5–8 classroom. The activities are particularly well suited to urban schools, where access to natural study sites such as lakes, streams, and forest trails, or even

small plots of grass, are limited. What's more, the focus on individual student observations and cooperative group work (rather than teacher-centered lectures, traditional textbooks, or pencil-and-paper tests) as the basis for conceptual understanding levels the playing field among students of different genders, cultures, and native languages.

As you acquaint yourself with this book, keep in mind that though classroom ready, these 20 activities are intended to be neither rigid nor overly prescriptive. Think of them as models or jumping off points, and let the active, constructivist approach to teaching inspire you to develop and implement your own academically integrated lessons that stimulate the natural curiosity and problem-solving skills of your students.

## Theoretical Foundation

Educational constructivists believe meaningful learning depends on prior experience (Piaget 1970). Understanding is mediated by personal and social background; knowledge is constructed, negotiated, and tested via experience. The only adequate test of knowledge, then, is its viability when applied to current problems (Tobin 1993). Constructivism does not outline a particular methodology but generally suggests that you consider students' prior experience (and even misconceptions), create situations in which students have opportunities to reconceptualize naive ideas, and remain flexible and alert to the growth and viability of student knowledge. As von Glasersfeld noted, "successful thinking is more important than 'correct' answers," and to foster motivation, the constructivist teacher will "create situations where the students have an opportunity to experience the pleasure inherent in solving a problem" (1993, p. 33). *ALSM* combines this attention to students' experience and successful thinking with classroom lessons and pedagogic strategies you will quickly recognize: hands-on and minds-on instruction, guided discovery, experimentation, the learning cycle, open-ended challenges, projects, metacognition, attention to the affective domain, and authentic assessment. (A matrix clarifying the various instructional strategies used in each of the activities appears on p. 12.) The activities described in the following pages are unique because they encourage the reader to apply well-known teaching techniques in somewhat novel, more student-centered ways.

Four overarching principles—each clearly recognized and encouraged by the national standards in science and mathematics—guide the activities in this book (AAAS 1989, 1993; NCTM 2000, 2006; NRC 1996).

1. *Student relevance* refers to a focus on student interests, prior knowledge, questions, and ideas, as well as student-initiated

projects and solutions. In short, lessons should reflect the lives of the students involved. In the words of the NSES, "Teachers [should] plan to meet the particular interests, knowledge, and skills of their students and build on their questions and ideas" (NRC 1996, p. 31). Relying only on teacher-directed memorization of facts is insufficient and ineffective according to a number of influential sources, including the national standards in science and mathematics (AAAS 1989, 1993; NCTM 2000; NRC 1996). If a deeper and more viable understanding is to be reached, educators must help students bridge the familiar with the unfamiliar. That is, meaningful teaching begins with what students already know and connects through active learning methods to new expansive concepts and understandings. *Principles and Standards for School Mathematics* states, "Mathematics makes more sense and is easier to remember and to apply when students connect new knowledge to existing knowledge in meaningful ways" (NCTM 2000, p. 20).

2.  *Interaction/collaboration* reflects the fact that elementary students are fundamentally concrete thinkers who require personal and interpersonal experiences to learn effectively (Vygotsky 1978). As the NSES explain, "Interactions among individuals and groups in the classroom can be vital in deepening the understanding of scientific concepts and the nature of scientific endeavors" (NRC 1996, p. 32). You should, therefore, actively involve students both personally and socially in science–math explorations. Engaging lessons that encourage involvement and provide opportunities for meaningful understanding are optimally motivating for students, especially in grades 5–8. We also know that to be fully effective, interactive studies must be undertaken in a collaborative manner. Learning depends on socialization, and a deep understanding of science and math depends on an awareness of the interpersonal aspects of those disciplines (Vygotsky 1978). Keep in mind that well-managed group work in the classroom closely resembles the collaborative nature of real-world science, mathematics, and technology—thus offering students authentic, interactive experiences (AAAS 1989; NRC 1996).

3.  *Problem-based learning* provides a challenging and motivating context for classroom math and science exploration. An essential feature of the current national standards in math and science education is a call for deeper, more active, and more relevant inquiry. "Well-chosen tasks can pique students' curiosity and draw them into mathematics," says the National Council of Teachers of Mathematics (NCTM

2000, p. 18). Posing realistic, interesting, open-ended, and challenging problems for students to solve is a mainstay of the reform movement. In particular, Meier, Hovde, and Meier (1996) stress the importance of realistic and interdisciplinary applications of problem solving. Through problem solving in the classroom, students learn to effectively confront real-life demands by applying higher-order thinking skills. Thus, the development of problem-solving skills through active, engaging investigation is fundamental to the national standards in science and mathematics (NCTM 2000; NRC 1996).

4. Integrated instruction is the blending of two or more academic disciplines into a particular classroom lesson. Science and mathematics, though traditionally treated in academia as discrete intellectual entities, are not separated in the real world. Integrated instruction not only promotes the presentation of the subjects in a realistic and relevant context but also provides opportunities for imaginative and personal connections between students and subject matter, further enhancing understanding and motivation. Cross-disciplinary connections deepen understanding by allowing students to simultaneously use the language, concepts, and methods of thinking of several subject areas. That is, students have an opportunity to view and comprehend a situation from more than one disciplinary perspective, generating a greater complexity of meaning (Fosnot 1996). Research into the impact of integrated science–math instruction shows a positive effect on student achievement, problem-solving ability, self-worth, motivation, and interest (Meier, Cobbs, and Nicol 1998). Finally, on a practical level, integrated instruction, by connecting subjects and thereby condensing teaching time, provides more time to teach science and math in what has become a very tight daily teaching schedule.

*Integrated, unified, blended, interdisciplinary, cross-disciplinary, multidisciplinary, thematic,* and *coordinated*—all are words used to describe simultaneous instruction in multiple disciplines. However, because these terms tend to be used inconsistently, there is a great deal of confusion about what they actually mean. Lederman and Neiss (1998) observe that integration, for example, tends to be used in one of two ways: First, it may refer to instructional situations in which traditional boundaries are blurred or even lost. Or, it may refer to situations that maintain traditional boundaries but stress the interaction among the disciplines during instruction. Lederman and Neiss favor the second definition, explaining that conventions differ between science and mathematics, largely due to the notion that sci-

ence (and not math) must consider external empirical observations in problem-solving situations. Ways of knowing vary significantly between science and mathematics (as well as between other academic disciplines), enabling educators to discriminate one discipline from another. Therefore, if students are to gain understanding of how science, math, or any other intellectual discipline functions, the lines separating the disciplines should not be erased or even significantly blurred. Rather than dissolving disciplines into incongruous hybrids, Lederman and Neiss argue that if you are interested in integrated instruction, you should help students find meaningful interconnections among existing disciplines. Although a certain amount of disciplinary "cloudiness" is bound to exist in any attempt at integrated instruction, the science–math links described in the activities in this book reflect the position of Lederman and Neiss.

## How to Use This Book

Think of *ALSM* not as an activity book but as an instructional framework and a resource that can be easily adapted to any discipline.[1] The activities can be introduced in any sequence and may be used in a variety of ways: as an active introduction or dynamic closure to a unit of study; as a motivational, guided inquiry that supplements the core curriculum via application; or as an open-ended and independent investigatory project. Choose activities that reflect and extend your required curriculum, or try one that looks appealing or taps into a particular student interest. Expand or modify the activities to meet your individual class needs and as time permits. Be mindful of opportunities that allow you to draw connections with past or future areas of study.

When implementing the activity ideas, plan thoroughly but remain open to emergent and spontaneous learning opportunities, paying particular attention to student questions, impressions, and proposals. Student ideas are often the keys to establishing meaningful understanding and lasting motivation. Listen carefully to students as they investigate, think, and grow in confidence and knowledge. Take your cues from them as you brainstorm how to improve your instruction and seek ways to extend lessons into new areas of learning. Remember, successful teachers prepare thoroughly, enjoy the experience, and share their joy of learning with students.

---

1 Francis and Underhill (1996) provide another practical approach for developing interdisciplinary lessons, one that may be applied effectively in most classrooms. Their model relies on collaboration between two teachers (one math, one science), determines the key components of each topic to be taught, and uses a matrix format to plan instructional connections between those key components.

# INTRODUCTION

This book is organized according to scientific discipline, as seen in the Table of Contents, to expedite the location of appropriate lesson ideas for your curriculum planning. In actuality, the various disciplines overlap substantially and many activities include aspects of several diverse science disciplines. For example, Activity 11: Exploring the Dynamics of Temperature, which is listed as a chemical science project, also involves a significant amount of biology and physics. Similarly, most activities have a great deal more math embedded in the procedure than can be conveniently outlined in each lesson's list of concepts.

Take advantage of the curricular ambiguity inherent in linking disciplines, as it provides for more malleable lessons. The amount of science, math, art, literature, and so on that you include in your lesson depends on your pedagogic style, curriculum needs, and comfort level with the material. Students' backgrounds, interests, and goals should also come into play. In short, the depth and breadth of interdisciplinary connections is entirely up to you and your class, thus allowing for a customization of experience and meaning.

The *ALSM* lesson structure essentially provides a framework for students to do much of their own exploring and discovering. Start by introducing an idea or concept via a question, demonstration, or simple activity. This technique both engages your class and allows you to check for background knowledge and interest in the topic. Then, together with your class, proceed through the activity step-by-step. Students, who are often broken into small cooperative groups, collect, analyze, and discuss data, then share their reactions and insights. You have no particular script to follow, but modeling inquiry and problem-solving strategies in your own approaches to the activities is highly encouraged. The step-by-step directions are specific enough for you to easily work through the activity, yet general enough to allow for adaptations as necessary.

## Assessment

Standardized or traditional assessment methods are usually inappropriate for evaluating integrated, problem-based tasks such as those that appear in this book. More suitable means of assessment have therefore been included for each activity. These methods may be termed *authentic assessment*, or methods of evaluation that are well matched to experiential tasks. These methods include the following:

1. *Embedded Assessment:* This technique blends conceptual assessment and instruction into a seamless whole, rather than following the traditional teach-test-teach-test format. This sort of observation is facilitated by asking students questions about their experiences as they

participate, such as "What if…?" or "Explain how you know…." For example, you can assess students' responses to an activity's Discussion Questions *while* they are actively investigating.

2. *Performance Tasks:* Evaluate how students apply their knowledge as they participate in science activities. You observe them actually doing science and their level of involvement, looking for mastery of desired skills, processes, and content understanding. For example, in Activity 1, Studies in Symmetry, determine whether or not students could classify the objects and photos into piles according to their symmetry.

3. *Journal Entries:* Journals are an effective means of integrating language arts into the study of science and math. In their journals, students can collect and analyze data, explain what they have learned, and reflect on their experiences. Entries could also include illustrations and sketches, enabling you to assess from a nonverbal angle.

Specific assessment suggestions, and associated evaluation rubrics, are provided in each activity. To gain a more complete perspective of student progress, use several means of assessment within a given lesson. Whatever means of evaluation you choose, however, the assessment must match the instructional task, meaning that as you evaluate students in these wide-ranging investigations, do more than simply assess vocabulary acquisition and concept memorization with conventional techniques.

## Safety Issues

During the implementation of the *ALSM* lessons, safety issues are of utmost importance. Use appropriate laboratory procedures while undertaking the activities, not only for the students' immediate safety, but also for the development of their lifelong safety habits. Specific safety considerations have been included in each activity, and *The NSTA Ready-Reference Guide to Safer Science* (Roy 2007) is an excellent resource for further reading. Essential safety recommendations include the following:

1. Keep the work area clean. Clean all spills immediately. Clean and store equipment and materials after use.

2. Never taste any chemicals. Always sniff gases cautiously. Store materials appropriately and safely.

3. Wear protective eyewear when working with hazardous substances or in any hazardous situations.

4. Be especially careful with electricity.

5. Provide constant supervision during individual or group work.

6. Allow sufficient time to complete tasks without rushing.

7. Provide sufficient lighting and ventilation.

8. Keep safety in mind when undertaking any *ALSM* or other investigatory activities.

It is vital to remember that, as stated in *The NSTA Ready-Reference Guide to Safer Science*, "the best piece of safety equipment in your classroom is you—the informed adult shaping and controlling the learning environment" (Roy 2007, p. xiii).

## Breaking Down Each Activity

The *ALSM* lesson format is broken into a number of sections, each providing important information at a glance. Before trying the activity in class, read the entire lesson to facilitate choices of questioning strategies, modifications, assessment, and overall implementation. Practicing the activity ahead of time also minimizes mistakes and confusion during the classroom presentation. What follows is an explanation of each section of the lesson format, as well as suggestions for use.

- **Overview:** A concise description of the activity that helps you determine where it may fit into your curriculum.

- **Processes/Skills:** A list of the processes and skills that students can be expected to employ as they participate in the activity.

- **Recommended For:** A recommended grade range is provided for each activity, but the activities can be easily adapted for either younger or older students. In general, for younger students, simplify the use of terminology, eliminate or adapt procedures requiring fine motor skills, break the duration of the inquiry into shorter segments, and be sure that the lesson proceeds in a clear, orderly, and sequential manner. For older students, expand on the terminology and concepts, provide deeper connections to other disciplines, and offer opportunities for individual exploration, perhaps extending to investigations that can be undertaken outside the classroom (e.g., home, neighborhood, museums). A recommendation for individual, small-group, or whole-class instruction is also given.

- **Time Required:** An approximate time range for completion of the activity; this will vary from class to class and should be considered only a rough estimate. Longer activities, or portions of activities, can be carried out over several days rather than all in one session.

- **Materials Required for Main Activity:** A list of what materials are needed for the Main Activity as well as for any follow-up activities. Gather and, when necessary, assemble all materials prior to teaching the lesson—nothing ruins a well-organized plan as quickly as a missing item.

- **Connecting to the Standards:** A list of the standards related to the activity. The standards are also noted in the margins of the Step-by-Step Procedures at their main points of use, though they may well apply in several locations within a given activity. Complete discussions of each standard can be found in *National Science Education Standards* (NRC 1996) and *Principles and Standards for School Mathematics* (NCTM 2000)

- **Safety Considerations:** A warning of potential safety issues associated with the lesson. Familiarize yourself with classroom safety procedures and policies.

- **Activity Objectives:** A statement of performance objectives that students can be expected to reach during the lesson.

- **Background Information:** Conceptual information and explanations of terminology, when needed. In some cases, background information is included within the Step-by-Step Procedures.

- **Main Activity, Step-by-Step Procedures:** Sequential and ready-to-implement steps that are adaptable to fit the needs of each classroom.

- **Discussion Questions:** A crucial aspect of the activities is paying close attention to your questioning strategy. Thought-provoking discussion questions are provided within the procedures and in this separate section following the procedures to promote the development of higher-order thinking skills, synthesis of disciplinary interconnections, and a deeper overall understanding. You should also develop your own queries, using a range of open- and closed-ended questions to stimulate students' critical thinking. Be careful not to dwell too much on or give away "the right answers," however, because an essential aspect of these lessons is that students have a chance to participate in the process of inquiry.

- **Assessment:** Several specific means of evaluating student progress and, in parentheses, suggestions for using the general method(s) of evaluation. Rubrics are provided for each lesson. In informal assessments, also include aspects of the affective domain, such as whether students are having fun, cooperating with one another, and acting interested.

- **Going Further:** For some lessons, a connecting activity to expand the basic lesson into another subject area, particularly the visual arts.

- **Other Options and Extensions:** Additional ideas for extending the basic activity. These can be pursued with the class as time allows, or they can be made available to individual students as homework, independent investigation, or a foundation for further study.

- **Resources:** Citations for articles, books, and other supplementary resources.

## Final Thoughts

It is, indeed, possible to maintain high academic standards while "loosening up" your curriculum to include the natural connections among disciplines. Interdisciplinary connections are not simply interesting side trips; rather, they represent the foundation for lifelong understanding, curiosity, and problem solving. Science and mathematics reinforce each other, each discipline drawing from the techniques and tools of the other and offering students experiences and awareness that are greater than the sum of the parts. By linking science with math we enhance comprehension and appreciation of both. Help students appreciate science and mathematics not only as topics to be studied in school, but also as vital, interrelated elements of their everyday lives.

## References

American Association for the Advancement of Science (AAAS). 1989. *Science for all Americans.* New York: Oxford University Press.

American Association for the Advancement of Science (AAAS). 1993. *Benchmarks for science literacy.* New York: Oxford University Press.

Fosnot, C. T. 1996. Constructivism: A psychological theory of learning. In *Constructivism: Theory, perspectives, and practice,* ed. C. T. Fosnot, 8–33. New York: Teachers College Press.

Francis, R., and R. G. Underhill. 1996. A procedure for integrating math and science units. *School Science and Mathematics* 96 (3): 114–119.

Lederman, N. G., and M. L. Neiss. 1998. 5 apples + 4 oranges = ? *School Science and Mathematics* 98 (6): 281–284.

McComas, W. F., and H. A. Wang. 1998. Blended science: The rewards and challenges of integrating the science disciplines for instruction. *School Science and Mathematics* 98 (6): 340–348.

Meier, S. L., G. Cobbs, and M. Nicol. 1998. Potential benefits and barriers to integration. *School Science and Mathematics* 98 (8): 438–445.

Meier, S. L., R. L. Hovde, and R. L. Meier. 1996. Problem solving: Teachers' perceptions, content area models, and interdisciplinary connections. *School Science and Mathematics* 96 (5): 230–237.

National Council of Teachers of Mathematics (NCTM). 2000. *Principles and standards for school mathematics*. Reston, VA: NCTM.

National Council of Teachers of Mathematics (NCTM). 2006. *Curriculum focal points for prekindergarten through grade 8 mathematics*. Reston, VA: NCTM.

National Research Council (NRC). 1996. *National science education standards*. Washington, DC: National Academy Press.

Piaget, J. 1970. *Genetic epistemology*. New York: Columbia University Press.

Roy, K. R. 2007. *The NSTA ready-reference guide to safer science*. Arlington, VA: NSTA Press.

Tobin, K., ed. 1993. *The practice of constructivism in science education*. Washington, DC: AAAS Press.

von Glasersfeld, E. 1993. Questions and answers about radical constructivism. In *The practice of constructivism in science education*, ed. K. Tobin, 23–38. Washington, DC: AAAS Press.

Vygotsky, L. S. 1978. *Mind in society: The development of higher psychological processes*. Cambridge, MA: Harvard University Press.

Whitehead, A. N. 1929. *The aims of education and other essays*. New York: Macmillan.

# KEY INSTRUCTIONAL STRATEGIES USED IN EACH ACTIVITY

| Activity | Hands-On | Minds-On | Guided Discovery | Experiment | Learning Cycle | Open-Ended Challenge | Project | Metacognition (Reflective Thinking) |
|---|---|---|---|---|---|---|---|---|
| 1 Symmetry | X | | X | | X | | | |
| 2 Internet/Science and Math | | X | | | | | X | X |
| 3 Current Events | | X | | | | | X | X |
| 4 Tower Challenge | X | | | | | X | | |
| 5 Load-Bearing Structure | X | | | | | X | | |
| 6 Investigating Cameras | X | | X | | | | | |
| 7 Pinhole Camera | X | | X | | | | | |
| 8 Levers | X | | X | X | X | | | |
| 9 Layered Liquids | X | | X | X | X | | | |
| 10 Speed of Sound | X | | X | | | | X | |
| 11 Dynamics of Temperature | X | | | X | | | | |
| 12 Acids and Bases | X | | | X | X | | | |
| 13 Sand | X | | | | | | | |
| 14 Heat Exchange | X | | | X | X | | | |
| 15 Earth Model | X | | | | X | | | |
| 16 Blind Spot | X | | X | | | | | |
| 17 Perception and Illusion | X | | X | | | | | |
| 18 Height and Hand Length | X | | | X | | | | X |
| 19 Cell Shape | X | | X | | | | | |
| 20 Pollen | X | | X | X | | | | |

NATIONAL SCIENCE TEACHERS ASSOCIATION

# Activity 1
### Studies in Symmetry

## Overview

This engaging lesson simultaneously involves animals, flowers, mathematical patterns, and art. Students will learn to discern between radial symmetry, bilateral symmetry, and asymmetry by observing and classifying objects, shapes, and photos and by determining their own rules for classifying according to symmetry. Options for creating several art projects demonstrating symmetry are also provided.

## Processes/Skills

- Observing
- Comparing
- Classifying
- Measuring
- Describing
- Identifying patterns
- Problem solving
- Developing spatial reasoning
- Reflecting

## Recommended For

*Grades 5–8: Small-group or whole-class instruction*
This activity can be adapted for students in grades 5 and 6 by offering more assistance during Procedures 3 through 5 and by simplifying the introduced vocabulary as necessary.

## Time Required

2–3 hours

## Materials Required for Main Activity

- An assortment of photos, shapes, and objects representing radial symmetry, bilateral symmetry, and asymmetry (rocks; shells; nuts and bolts; flowers; plastic bottles; garlic cloves; any sorts of bones; photos of living things such as jellyfish, mammals, apples, insects)

- Several hand mirrors (plastic, not glass)

- Plain and colored paper

- Scissors

- Metric rulers

## Materials Required for Going Further

- Tempera paint

- Small plastic bowls to hold paint

- String

- Basic art supplies

## Connecting to the Standards

### NSES
#### Grade 5–8 Content Standards:
Standard A: Science as Inquiry

- Abilities necessary to do scientific inquiry (especially observing carefully, thinking critically about evidence to develop and communicate good explanations, and using mathematics effectively)

- Understanding about scientific inquiry (especially recognizing the importance of mathematics in science and noticing that scientific explanations emphasize evidence and logically consistent arguments)

Standard C: Life Science

- Structure and function in living systems (especially recognizing the complementary nature of structure and function)

- Diversity and adaptations of organisms (especially understanding

that structural adaptations allow organisms to successfully survive and reproduce)

## NCTM
### Standards for Grades 3–8:

- Geometry (especially identifying, naming, and/or comparing two-dimensional shapes, and applying geometric ideas in science and art)

- Problem Solving (especially constructing new math knowledge through problem solving, and applying strategies to solve a mathematical problem)

- Connections (especially applying mathematics to contexts outside mathematics)

- Representation (especially applying mathematical representations to model and solve problems)

# Safety Considerations
Basic classroom safety practices apply. Use plastic, rather than glass, mirrors.

# Activity Objectives
In this activity, students

- classify objects and shapes according to their symmetry;

- develop specific rules that allow them to sort shapes based on symmetry; and

- apply their understanding of symmetry by constructing symmetrical objects of their own design, including snowflakes and flowers.

# Background Information
Symmetry refers to the shape of an object and is defined as the state of having balanced proportions. In this activity we will be concerned with *bilateral symmetry*, in which a median plane divides the object into two sides, and *radial symmetry*, in which there is a balance of parts around a central point. We could say that a bilaterally symmetrical object has right and left, upper and lower, or back and front halves, and that the halves are mirror images of each other. We could say that a radially symmetrical object radiates out, for 360°, around a central point. Orchids, insects, and humans exhibit bilateral symmetry, whereas daisies, sea urchins, and

**STUDIES IN SYMMETRY**

starfish exhibit radial symmetry. Objects that are not balanced are said to be *asymmetrical*.

## Main Activity, Step-by-Step Procedures

1. Begin the lesson by showing the students a wide variety of objects and photos, and ask, "When we consider shape, how is a jellyfish like a daisy? How is a butterfly like an orchid?" There are two ways to proceed at this point, depending on time constraints and the number of objects/photos available. One option is to divide the class into cooperative groups and have each group sort the objects/ photos into different piles based on the shapes of the objects. The other option is for you to categorize the objects/photos into piles and to challenge the students to decide what your criteria were for the sorting process. The first option is hands-on, the second more of a "minds-on" demonstration, but both should encourage divergent thinking and analysis of the shapes presented.

2. Proceed by introducing the terms *symmetry, bilateral symmetry, radial symmetry*, and *asymmetry*. Be sure that the students understand which of the objects observed in Procedure 1 demonstrate these concepts. The terms will be particularly meaningful to the students if you help them connect the concepts and terms with their efforts and experiences in Procedure 1. That is, you might say something like, "I notice that Group 3 separated several objects (jellyfish, daisy, pie) into a pile. Do you see that all these objects, in addition to being round, are radially symmetrical because they all radiate from a central point, unlike the bilaterally symmetrical or asymmetrical objects?" Or, "Did any groups classify objects into an 'unusual shape' pile, an 'unbalanced' pile? Well, those objects were unbalanced, or asymmetrical."

    Now let the groups (or the entire class, if you're doing this as a demonstration) reclassify the objects/photos into radially symmetrical, bilaterally symmetrical, and asymmetrical piles, visiting each group and checking for comprehension as they proceed. Then direct the students—in groups or as a class—to make three lists of objects and/or organisms *other than* those included in Procedure 1 that are radially symmetrical, bilaterally symmetrical, or asymmetrical (see Activity Sheet 1.1, p. 25). You could list a few objects/organisms on the board to get the ball rolling (such as cow, cloud, grasshopper, oak tree, acorn, or stapler). Discuss the lists as a class, noticing which list was difficult, which was easy, and why.

**3.** Ask the class to name some geometric shapes and to determine which of the three categories each shape belongs in. You can facilitate this by making cardboard cutout shapes ahead of time and presenting a set to each cooperative group of students. Include various triangles, circles, ovals, parallelograms, trapezoids, and so on. You could also include numerical relationships, such as equations, or graphic portrayals, such as a parabola on a graph, as an extra challenge.

Next, consider just the organism photos from Procedure 1 and the organisms listed in Activity Sheet 1.1. How do the shapes (asymmetrical or symmetrical) of living things help them to survive? Their shapes represent biological adaptations that enhance some aspect(s) of survival. Discuss how this is true for each organism. For example, the daisy's radial symmetry makes the flower easy for a bee to locate and land on, which encourages successful pollination. An insect's bilateral symmetry allows it to fly or walk effectively, which enhances feeding and reproductive behaviors, as well other aspects of survival.

**4.** Some objects may appear to be both bilaterally and radially symmetrical. A two-liter plastic bottle, for example, is bilaterally symmetrical if viewed from the side, and radially symmetrical if viewed from either end. Give each student group several objects/photos from each of the three categories, and challenge them to develop specific rules that will allow them to determine radial symmetry versus bilateral symmetry versus asymmetry. Encourage a diversity of solutions to the challenge. As a class, consider each group's rules and decide if those rules will work for any object presented. Discuss the advantages and disadvantages of the various rules presented. To add an extra dimension to the search for symmetry rules, you could give each group a small hand mirror along with their objects. Can the instrument (i.e., the mirror) be an aid in developing rules for symmetry? By placing an object partially behind the mirror and using the mirror's edge as a plane to "split" the object, the object's form of symmetry may be determined: (a) it is *bilaterally symmetrical* if it can only be split into two halves along only one central plane (see Figure 1.1, p. 18), (b) it is *radially symmetrical* if it can be split in any plane that goes through its center or its long axis (see Figure 1.2, p. 18), and (c) it is *asymmetrical* if there is no plane along which it may be evenly split (see Figure 1.3, p. 18).

**MATH**
Geometry
Representation

**SCIENCE**
Structure and function in
living systems

**MATH**
Problem solving
Connections

**STUDIES IN SYMMETRY**

**FIGURE 1.1.**
**Bilateral symmetry**

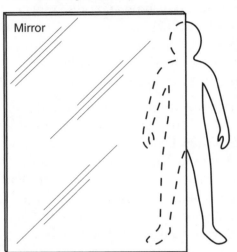

**FIGURE 1.2.**
**Radial symmetry**

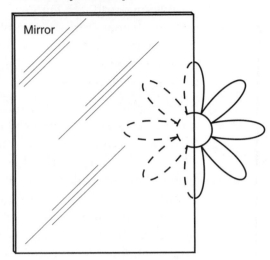

**FIGURE 1.3. Asymmetry**

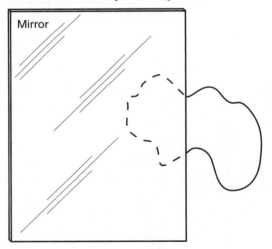

5. Next, you can include an art-related mathematical application of the symmetry concept. Instruct students to fold a piece of paper in half, and then draw half of a snowflake, flower, or Sun shape along the edge with the fold (see Figure 1.4). First ask, "If you cut along the line through both halves of the paper, will the resulting image be radially symmetrical, bilaterally symmetrical, or asymmetrical? How do you know? If the drawing you made is 10 cm from the fold to its widest point, how wide will the cutout, unfolded figure be?

How do you know?" Have students measure the width of the folded drawing before cutting, and have them predict the final, unfolded width of their snowflake/Sun/flower. Let them proceed to cut and measure. Check their results and the reactions to their predictions. Because these cutouts were folded into right and left halves, they should demonstrate bilateral symmetry.

**FIGURE 1.4. Folded figure**

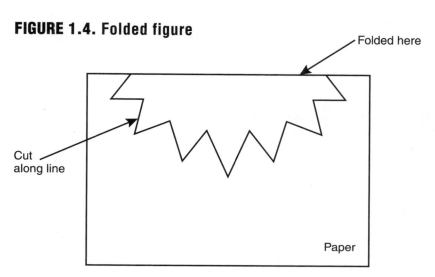

You can repeat the same basic activity, this time folding the paper in half twice instead of just once, and drawing a quarter of a snowflake, flower, or Sun shape along the edge with the fold. Repeat again, folding the paper in half three times and drawing an eighth of a snowflake, flower, or Sun along the edge with the fold. Ask students if they see the relationship between the number of folds in the paper and the fraction of the object represented. That is, one fold—one-half of the object, two folds—one-fourth of the object, three folds—one-eighth of the object. Based on this evidence, what fraction of the object would be drawn after making four folds? Five folds? Here are examples:

One fold,

$$\frac{1}{2^1} = \frac{1}{2}$$

Two folds,

$$\frac{1}{2^2} = \frac{1}{4}$$

Can your students discover this relationship on their own? How did they discover it and how did they express it?

6. Now introduce an open-ended problem (i.e., one that has more than one feasible solution). Ask students, in small groups, to design and construct a paper cutout or a collage/mosaic of a radially symmetrical flower that is adapted to a specific environment (e.g., rain forest, desert, mountain, prairie). Have students keep written records of their methods of construction. When all groups have finished, ask each to display its flower, tell where and how it might grow, and explain the method of construction to the class.

## Discussion Questions

Ask students the following:

1. How do radial symmetry, bilateral symmetry, and asymmetry differ?

2. Why is symmetry important in the study of animals and plants?

3. How is symmetry related to mathematics?

4. Consider the symmetry of plants and animals. How do the shapes of living things help them to survive?

5. How would your life be different if nothing were symmetrical? If everything were symmetrical?

6. How would you complete this sentence: Of all the symmetrical objects or living things that I know, the most beautiful is the _____ because _____.

## Assessment

Suggestions for specific ways to assess student understanding are provided in parentheses.

1. Were students able to classify the objects and photos into piles according to their symmetry? (Use Procedure 2 as a performance task and Discussion Question 1 as an embedded assessment.)

2. Were students able to classify the geometric shapes into piles according to their symmetry? (Use Procedure 3 as a performance task and Discussion Questions 1 and 3 as an embedded assessment.)

3. Were students able to see symmetry as a form of biological adaptation for living things? (Use Procedure 6 as a performance assessment and Discussion Question 4 as a prompt for a science journal entry.)

4. Were students able to develop specific rules that allowed them to differentiate between radial symmetry, bilateral symmetry, and asymmetry? (Use Procedure 4 as a performance task or as a prompt for a science journal entry.)

5. Did students successfully make folded-over snowflakes? Were they able to predict the symmetry and width of the snowflake image? (Use student outcomes during Procedure 5 as a performance assessment and responses to Discussion Questions 3 and 5 as embedded assessments.)

6. Were student groups able to construct a cutout or a collage/mosaic of a radially symmetrical flower? Could they explain their rationale and method of construction? (Use observed student activity as embedded evidence and Discussion Questions 2, 4, and 6 as science journal entries.)

**STUDIES IN SYMMETRY**

**RUBRIC 1.1**
**Sample rubric using these assessment options**

| | Achievement Level | | |
|---|---|---|---|
| | **Developing**<br>**1** | **Proficient**<br>**2** | **Exemplary**<br>**3** |
| Were students able to classify the objects and photos into piles according to their symmetry? | Unsuccessfully attempted to separate into piles based on symmetry | Successfully separated into piles based on symmetry | Successfully separated into piles based on symmetry and were able to explain in depth |
| Were students able to classify the geometric shapes into piles according to their symmetry? | Unsuccessfully attempted to separate into piles based on symmetry | Successfully separated into piles based on symmetry | Successfully separated into piles based on symmetry and were able to explain in depth |
| Were students able to see symmetry as a form of biological adaptation for living things? | Attempted to explain the value of symmetry as a biological adaptation, but unable to do so to any significant extent | Generally explained the value of symmetry as a biological adaptation | Explained in depth, with examples, the value of symmetry as a biological adaptation |
| Were students able to develop specific rules that allowed them to differentiate between radial symmetry, bilateral symmetry, and asymmetry? | Unsuccessfully attempted to develop rules to differentiate between the forms of symmetry | Successfully developed rules to differentiate between the forms of symmetry | Successfully developed rules to differentiate between the forms of symmetry and applied those rules to a variety of examples |
| Did students successfully make folded-over snowflakes? Were they able to predict the symmetry and width of the snowflake image? | Unsuccessfully attempted to make folded-over snowflakes | Successfully made folded-over snowflakes and predicted the snowflakes' widths and images | Successfully made folded-over snowflakes, predicted the snowflakes' widths and images, and could explain their predictions in detail, using appropriate terminology |
| Were student groups able to construct a cutout or a collage/mosaic of a radially symmetrical flower? Could they explain their rationales and methods of construction? | Unsuccessfully attempted to construct a collage/mosaic of a radially symmetrical flower | Successfully constructed a flower collage/mosaic and adequately explained the process | Successfully constructed a flower collage/mosaic and thoroughly explained the process, using appropriate terminology |

# Going Further

This project involves symmetry and painting. Explain to students that they are going to fold over a piece of paper (colored paper if available), place a piece of paint-saturated string (which was dipped into wet tempera paint) inside the folded-over paper, press on the paper while the string is inside, and then pull out the string while still pressing lightly on the paper. Ask

them to predict whether the resulting painting, when unfolded, will be radially symmetrical, bilaterally symmetrical, or asymmetrical.

The paper can be trimmed in interesting ways along the edge (before or after folding, or while folded), and the string can be pulled out either from the edge of the paper or through a small slit cut along the fold (see Figure 1.5). Various cords with interesting texture work well in this project. Several different strings with different color paints can be used on each painting. Students may also want to add dots, lines, or new patterns after unfolding.

**FIGURE 1.5. String and paper painting**

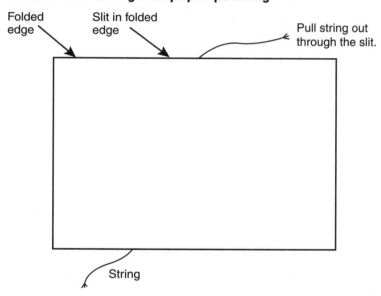

When these projects are completed, ask each student to write about what the resulting pattern reminds him or her of and why. How would the results differ if their symmetry differed? Display student work, with the permission of the artist(s).

## Other Options and Extensions

1. Homework: Challenge students to make drawings and/or descriptions of radially symmetrical, bilaterally symmetrical, and asymmetrical objects found in or near their homes. Students should bring the documented observations to class and compare them with those found by the other students.

2. Have students make a butterfly mosaic using colored paper, tile, and colored macaroni (soaked for a time in food coloring diluted with

water and then allowed to dry). Ask, "Is the butterfly symmetrical? Bilateral or radial?" Then have students explain how a butterfly's life might be different if it were radially symmetrical or asymmetrical.

3. Ask students, "Are we bilaterally symmetrical inside? What organs do we have two of? Which organs do we only have one of?" Answers should be written and then shared with the class.

## Resources

Beckstead, L. 2008. Scientific journals: A creative assessment. *Science and Children* 46 (3): 22–26.

Bidwell, J. K. 1987. Using reflections to find symmetric and asymmetric patterns. *The Arithmetic Teacher* 34 (1): 10–15.

Bricker, P. 2007. Reinvigorating science journals. *Science and Children* 45 (3): 24–29.

McDuffie, T. 2007. Precipitation matters. *Science and Children* 44 (9): 38–42.

Moyer, P. S. 2001. Patterns and symmetry, Reflections of culture. *Teaching Children Mathematics* 8 (3): 140–148.

Robertson, B. 2008. Science 101: Why do we classify things in science? *Science and Children* 45 (5): 70–72.

Schoffel, J. L., and M. L. Breyfogle. 2005. Reflecting shapes: Same or different? *Teaching Children Mathematics* 11 (7): 378–382.

Seidel, J. D. 1998. Symmetry in season. *Teaching Children Mathematics* 4 (5): 244–249.

Toll, D., and S. Stump. 2007. Characteristics of shapes. *Teaching Children Mathematics* 13 (9): 472–473.

**ACTIVITY SHEET 1.1**
**Learning Cycle Studies in Symmetry**

Make a list of objects or living organisms that demonstrate the following:

| Radial Symmetry | Bilateral Symmetry | Asymmetry |
|---|---|---|
| | | |
| | | |
| | | |
| | | |
| | | |
| | | |
| | | |

# +General Science

# Activity 2

## Surveying Science and Mathematics on the Internet

## Overview

In this activity, students will explore the internet for interesting science and mathematics websites. They will be guided by an activity sheet as they identify, summarize, analyze, reflect on, and compare websites. After reviewing their sites, students will have an opportunity to present their findings to the class, providing the teacher with a chance to lead the class toward a deeper understanding of the internet and what it can offer. This is a valuable lesson for students whose very livelihoods may someday depend on their ability to navigate online information resources.

## Processes/Skills

- Describing
- Analyzing
- Concluding
- Inferring
- Inquiring
- Communicating

## Recommended For

*Grades 5–8: Individual, small-group, or whole-class instruction*
While older students will be more familiar with searching the web for science and math sites, students in grades 5–6 may need to be steered specifically toward one or more of the sites listed below or in the Internet Resources at the back of this book (see p. 207).

## Time Required

1–2 hours

## Materials Required for Main Activity

- Computer(s) with internet connection

## Connecting to the Standards

### NSES
**Grade 5–8 Content Standards:**

Standard A: Science as Inquiry

- Abilities necessary to do scientific inquiry (especially using the appropriate technological tools for successful scientific investigations)

Standard E: Science and Technology

- Understanding about science and technology (especially that technology is essential to science, providing tools for inquiry and analysis)

### NCTM
**Standards for Grades 3–8:**

- Communication (especially analyzing and evaluating the mathematical thinking of others)
- Connections (especially recognizing the connections among mathematical ideas and to investigations outside mathematics)

## Safety Considerations

Basic classroom safety practices apply. Be certain to monitor student web use to avoid contact with inappropriate sites and information.

## Activity Objectives

In this activity, students

- successfully identify, summarize, analyze, and compare science-related and/or math-related websites.

## Background Information

The key component in this activity is student access to the internet. Students may gain access through computers in your classroom, the school computer lab, the school library, a public library, at home, or at the home of a friend, neighbor, or family member. An internet connection must be made available to all class members. If computer access is limited, let students work on the

project in groups, and/or carry out this activity on a contractual basis. That is, all students or groups won't be working on this activity at the same time; you can spread the assignment over a week, a month, or the entire semester. The activity also presupposes that your students have some experience in finding and using websites on the internet.

Examples of appropriate websites for this activity include the following:

Exploratorium—The Museum of Science, Art and Human Perception: *www.exploratorium.edu* (also has links to "Ten Cool Sites")

Math2.org: *http://math2.org* (see links, too)

The Yuckiest Site on the Internet: *http://yucky.discovery.com/flash*

Project Dragonfly: *www.units.muohio.edu/dragonfly*

Beautiful Birds—Masterpieces From the Hill Ornithology Collection: *http://rmc.library.cornell.edu/ornithology/frames/exhibit.htm*

Ocean Remote Sensing Group Image Gallery: *http://fermi.jhuapl.edu/avhrr/gallery*

Totally Tessellated: *http://library.thinkquest.org/16661/index2.html*

## Main Activity, Step-by-Step Procedures

1.  Ask students what they know about the internet. Has anyone ever used a math or science site? What was their purpose in locating the site? What did they find there?

    Explain to the class that this activity involves the internet. Challenge students to identify, explore, analyze, and report on a website that meets the following criteria:

    -   It is related to science, mathematics, an integration of science and mathematics, an integration of science and some other school subject, or an integration of mathematics and some other school subject.

    -   It is interesting to you (the student).

2.  Provide individual students or small student groups with sufficient time and computer access (see Background Information) to complete Activity Sheet 2.1, p. 32. It is preferable for students to do this activity on school computers because then you can observe, monitor, facilitate, and assess their work.

3.  Once students have explored their websites and have completed their written reports, provide them with an opportunity to share

**SCIENCE**
Abilities necessary to do scientific inquiry
Understanding about science and technology

**MATH**
Communication
Connections

their findings with the class. You can expand their analyses by asking, "Would you add anything to this site? Subtract anything? What questions do you have about the site you visited?" Allow students to share their excerpts and graphics in small groups, and then lead them in a comparison of the various sites explored. Address the following questions in your discussion: How did the excerpts compare? How did the graphics compare? Which sites would students revisit? For older or more advanced students, you can ask more reflective questions, such as, "Who authored this site and how might the author's position bias the site's perspective?"

## Discussion Questions

Ask students the following:

1. How did the various websites compare? How were they similar? How were they different?

2. If you could reorganize the site that you visited, what would you change?

3. If you were going to start your own science or math website, what would you call it, what sort of information would it contain, and how would it look?

## Assessment

Suggestions for specific ways to assess student understanding are provided in parentheses.

1. Were students able to successfully identify, summarize, analyze, and compare science-related and/or math-related websites? (Use Activity Sheet 2.1 as a performance assessment, and use responses to Discussion Questions 1–3 as embedded evidence or as prompts for science journal entries.)

**RUBRIC 2.1**
**Sample rubric using this assessment option**

| | Achievement Level | | |
|---|---|---|---|
| | Developing 1 | Proficient 2 | Exemplary 3 |
| Were students able to successfully identify, summarize, analyze, and compare science-related and/or math-related websites? | Were not able to locate science-related and/or math-related websites | Were able to successfully identify and summarize science-related and/or math-related websites | Were able to successfully identify, summarize, analyze, and compare science-related and/or math-related websites |

## Other Options and Extensions

Try an internet scavenger hunt. Challenge students, working in teams or as individuals, to find as many of the following websites as possible (for each site, they must write a brief description and list the full web address):

- Site with information about butterflies

- Site dealing with geometry

- Site of your state's weather

- Site with pictures of the Moon

- Site that tells you something about the abacus

- Site with Uruguay's weather

- Site dealing with mathematics in Africa

- Site with information about bridges

- Site containing data about rain forest research

## Resources

Ebeneezer, J. V., and E. Lau. 1999. *Science on the Internet: A resource for K–12 teachers*. Upper Saddle River, NJ: Merrill.

O'Brien, G. E., and S. P. Lewis. 1999. Connecting to resources on the Internet. *Science and Children* 36 (8): 42–45.

Smith, S. W. 2000. Get connected to science! *Science and Children* 37 (7): 22–25.

Timmerman, M. 2004. Using the Internet: Are prospective elementary teachers prepared to teach with technology? *Teaching Children Mathematics* 10 (8): 410–415.

### ACTIVITY SHEET 2.1
### Surveying Science and Mathematics on the Internet

Name of Website:

Internet Address:

Please answer the following:

1. What information is available at this site?

2. Why is the site important? Or, to whom might it be important?

3. Why did you choose this site? What interested you?

4. Is the site basically science, math, or a combination? Explain your answer.

5. Is there anything that you would change about this website, and if so, what?

6 Do you have any questions about the information presented on the site, or about the site itself? If so, list those questions here.

7. Choose an excerpt from the site that you find particularly interesting. Print it and attach it to this report. Why did you choose this particular excerpt?

8. Print out a graphic, graph, or table from the site that you find particularly interesting. Attach it to this report. Why did you choose this particular graphic?

9. Would you recommend this site to a friend? Why or why not?

# +General Science

# Activity 3

## Examining Current Events in Science, Mathematics, and Technology

## Overview

The national standards in science and mathematics call for these subjects to be taught from personal and social perspectives, thus strengthening students' decision-making skills. Preeminent science educator Paul DeHart Hurd called for "a curriculum that relates science to human affairs, the quality of life, and social progress" (1994, p. 109). In this activity students will examine news articles not only from the perspective of science, math, and technology, but also based on the implications of the news story for its impact on real people, that is, based on human rights and social justice. Interdisciplinary connections are embedded in an engaging, accessible, and human context, as students read, analyze, and openly discuss a teacher-selected news article. By facilitating honest dialogue, the teacher helps students confidently face controversial topics and develop crucial critical-thinking skills.

## Processes/Skills

- Describing
- Analyzing
- Concluding
- Inferring
- Inquiring
- Communicating

## Recommended For

*Grades 5–8: Individual, small-group, or whole-class instruction*
By choosing news articles appropriate to students' ages and ability levels, this activity can be adjusted for any student in these grades.

**EXAMINING CURRENT EVENTS IN SCIENCE, MATHEMATICS, AND TECHNOLOGY**

## Time Required

1–2 hours

## Materials Required for Main Activity

- Enough photocopies of a news article for the entire class (consider newspaper, magazine, and internet sources)

## Connecting to the Standards

### NSES
**Grade 5–8 Content Standards:**

Standard A: Science as Inquiry

- Abilities necessary to do scientific inquiry (especially using appropriate tools to gather data, thinking critically, and considering alternative explanations)

Standard E: Science and Technology

- Understandings about science and technology (especially that perfectly designed technological solutions do not exist)

Standard G: History and Nature of Science

- Nature of science (especially that thorough evaluation and interpretation of investigations is a crucial part of scientific inquiry)

### NCTM
**Standards for Grades 3–8:**

- Communication (especially analyzing and evaluating the mathematical thinking of others)

- Connections (especially recognizing the connections among mathematical ideas and to investigations outside mathematics)

## Safety Considerations

Basic classroom safety practices apply. If students use online sources, be certain to monitor student web use to avoid contact with inappropriate sites and information.

## Activity Objectives

In this activity, students

- read and analyze a current event not only for its content in science, math, and/or technology, but also for its human impact, including human rights and social justice implications.

## Main Activity, Step-By-Step Procedures

1.  Begin by choosing a current event article from a newspaper or news magazine. The article should be directly relevant to some aspect of science, math, and/or technology. Because real-world issues seldom fall conveniently under a single subject heading, your article is likely to have indirect connections to other fields. Your choice of current events could raise issues and questions related to history, sociology, psychology, or politics. Be sure to exercise sensitivity to school district policies and community perspectives when choosing a news item. As you make your choice of articles, you might also consider the human rights issues associated with the news event. Such issues are not beyond the scope of the elementary or middle school classroom and are, in fact, highly motivating for students due to the relevance of the topics and the opportunities for authentic dialogue. Take into account the human rights issues associated with news stories regarding global climate change, immunization, cloning, colonization of other planets, organ transplants, environmental hazards, health care, or waste management. An integrated analysis of the news article, including consideration of human rights issues, is promoted by Activity Sheet 3.1, p. 39.

2.  Photocopy the article for all class members and read it together, clarifying new concepts and terms as necessary. Have students break into small groups for analysis of the article, with each individual student recording responses on Activity Sheet 3.1. Facilitate the analysis by moving around the room from group to group, listening, asking, and assessing.

3.  Resume whole-class instruction by discussing the groups' results and reactions to the article. Throughout the analysis and discussion, prompt students to notice and express their personal responses to the article. Encourage an awareness and use of authentic student voice, keeping in mind that this activity is designed to illuminate student perspectives via intellectual exploration, not simply to generate standardized, right/wrong responses. Personalize the discussion,

**SCIENCE**
Abilities necessary to do
  scientific inquiry

**MATH**
Connections

**SCIENCE**
Understanding about
  science and technology
Nature of science

**MATH**
Communication

especially at the elementary level; for example, ask "How might a young person like you react to these conditions?" Ask students to consider the article's impact on various demographic groups.

A basic approach to this analysis and discussion is as follows:

**a.** Clarify the problem. What is going on? Broaden students' understanding of the situation.

**b.** Define the basic pro and con reactions to the article, concentrating on science, math, and technology connections.

**c.** Consider the human rights implications: violations, infringements, advancements. Who is affected by the situation, and how are they affected?

**d.** Through open dialogue, determine workable solutions to the problem. Determine areas of impasse.

**e.** What must be done to implement the solution(s)?

**f.** What additional information is needed to help solve the problem?

The teacher has a number of responsibilities in this activity: to help students understand that every problem may not have a simple answer, to learn to accept an element of uncertainty, to seek fairness in presenting and discussing the topic, to avoid proselytization and the tendency to oversimplify complex topics, and ultimately to induce authentic, critical thought.

## Discussion Questions

Ask students the following:

**1.** Do all situations in real life have simple solutions? Explain your answer.

**2.** When faced with a complex problem, is it a good idea to consider more than one perspective before making any decisions? Explain your answer.

**3.** What sorts of careers might involve solving complex problems?

## Assessment

Suggestions for specific ways to assess student understanding are provided in parentheses.

**1.** Were students able to summarize the chosen article? (Use student responses to Activity Sheet 3.1 as a performance assessment and observations made during Procedure 3 as embedded evidence.)

2. Could students explain the importance of the article in terms of its science, technology, and/or math content? (Use student responses to Activity Sheet 3.1 as a performance assessment and observations made during Procedure 3 as embedded evidence.)

3. Were students able to discuss the human rights aspects of the current event? (Use observations made during Procedure 3 as embedded evidence.)

4. Did students, through open dialogue, arrive at solutions to the problem, or could they explain why a solution is not yet feasible? (Use observations made during Procedure 3 and student responses to the Discussion Questions as embedded evidence.)

**RUBRIC 3.1**
**Sample rubric using these assessment options**

| | Achievement Level | | |
| --- | --- | --- | --- |
| | Developing 1 | Proficient 2 | Exemplary 3 |
| Were students able to summarize the chosen article? | Attempted unsuccessfully to summarize the article | Summarized the article in a general way | Successfully summarized the article, including details and varying viewpoints |
| Could students explain the importance of the article in terms of its science, technology, and/or math (STEM) content? | Attempted unsuccessfully to explain the importance of STEM content | Generally explained the importance of STEM content | Explained the importance of STEM content in detail, noting interdisciplinary connections |
| Were students able to discuss the human rights aspects of the current event? | Attempted unsuccessfully to consider the article's human rights aspects | Generally considered the article's human rights aspects | Discussed the article's human rights aspects in detail, including viewpoints of different people |
| Did students, through open dialogue, arrive at solutions to the problem, or could they explain why a solution is not yet feasible? | Attempted unsuccessfully to arrive at a solution to the problem presented | Successfully described a solution to the problem presented | Successfully described several solutions to the problem and/or explained why solutions are not yet fully feasible |

# Other Options and Extensions

1. Students, either individually or in groups, might wish to expand their knowledge about the news topic. Encourage them to present their research to the class in the form of a debate, a play, a poem, a video, or an art project.

2. Have students write letters related to the news report. They should

# EXAMINING CURRENT EVENTS IN SCIENCE, MATHEMATICS, AND TECHNOLOGY

address the letters to parties in or related to the current event article *and actually send them.* Be judicious about sharing your own perspective so that your students will more readily develop and record their own views. This exercise is especially empowering when the news issue is local and students can see the results of their correspondence.

**3.** Have students explore news sources for relevant articles of their own choosing. Let them present and discuss those articles in groups or in a classwide forum.

## Resources

Hurd, P. D. 1994. New minds for a new age: Prologue to modernizing the science curriculum. *Science Education* 78 (1): 103–116.

Jennings, T. E., and J. Eichinger. 1999. Science education and human rights: Explorations into critical social consciousness and postmodern science instruction. *International Journal of Educational Reform* 8 (1): 37–44.

LeBeau, S. 1997. Newspaper mathematics. *Teaching Children Mathematics* 3 (5): 240–241.

McLaren, P. 1995. *Critical pedagogy and predatory culture: Oppositional politics in a postmodern era*. New York: Routledge.

O'Connell, S. R. 1995. Newspapers: Connecting the mathematics classroom to the world. *Teaching Children Mathematics* 1 (5): 268–274.

Silbey, R. 1999. What is in the daily news? *Teaching Children Mathematics* 5 (7): 390–394.

**GENERAL SCIENCE**

## ACTIVITY SHEET 3.1
### Examining Current Events in Science, Mathematics, and Technology

Respond to the following based on the news article from class.

**1.** Summarize the article in 30 to 50 words. List any new words that you don't understand.

**2.** What does the article have to do with science, math, or technology?

**3.** Who might be affected by the situation or problem reported in the article? How might they be affected?

**4.** Why is the article important? (Consider the viewpoints of several different people.)

**5.** What additional information is needed to resolve the problem reported in the article?

# + Physical Science

# Activity 4
## The Tower Challenge

## Overview

This activity is an exciting and highly interactive opportunity for students to exercise their creativity and design skills. Working in cooperative groups, students are challenged to explore the geometry of tower design and construction, first by experimenting with possible designs, and then by choosing the most likely design candidate and building the tallest tower possible, using only paper and tape. This activity is easily connected to social studies via discussion of the world's tall towers or to human anatomy via discussion of the long bones of the body (which act like towers).

## Processes/Skills

- Observing
- Measuring
- Describing
- Inferring
- Experimenting
- Communicating
- Developing spatial reasoning
- Constructing
- Comparing
- Reflecting
- Recognizing shapes and patterns
- Problem solving

## Recommended For

*Grades 5–8: Small-group instruction*
Adjust for grades 5 and 6 by considering the specific shapes of tall towers in detail during Procedure 1.

## Time Required

1–2 hours

## Materials Required for Main Activity

- Standard 8.5 × 11 inch paper (two different colors)
- Masking tape
- Metersticks
- Scissors

## Connecting to the Standards

### NSES
#### Grade 5–8 Content Standards:

Standard A: Science as Inquiry

- Abilities necessary to do scientific inquiry (especially thinking critically, using evidence, and applying mathematics)
- Understandings about scientific inquiry (especially emphasizing the value of evidence and mathematics)

Standard E: Science and Technology

- Abilities of technological design (especially identifying, implementing, and evaluating a design solution)
- Understanding about science and technology (especially that science and technology work together, and that technological designs have limitations)

### NCTM
#### Standards for Grades 3–8:

- Geometry (especially identifying, naming, comparing, and applying three-dimensional shapes)
- Measurement (especially understanding and applying the metric system)

- Problem Solving (especially applying strategies to solve problems)

- Reasoning and Proof (especially engaging in thinking and reasoning)

## Safety Considerations

Basic classroom safety practices apply.

## Activity Objectives

In this activity, students

- successfully design, construct, and evaluate free-standing paper towers;

- measure towers accurately and recognize geometric shapes in their tower designs; and

- compare their paper towers to famous or familiar towers of the world.

## Main Activity, Step-by-Step Procedures

1. Brainstorm with students. Start by asking, "What towers have you seen or visited?" Consider famous towers (e.g., Eiffel Tower, Watts Towers, Leaning Tower of Pisa), skyscrapers, radio transmission towers, and natural towers (e.g., Devils Tower in Wyoming). Point out to students that all "towers" are not necessarily architectural; for example, the long bones of the body such as the humerus and the femur are essentially towers, too. Ask, "What do towers have in common? How are they constructed? If you notice different tower 'varieties,' how would you categorize them?" Leave the brainstormed list(s) on the board during the activity to prompt speculation, experimentation, and creativity during tower construction. Be sure that students are considering a wide range of geometric options (in terms of the cross-sectional and vertical shapes of their towers) as they evaluate possible designs.

2. Tell students that you are challenging them to build their own towers in class. The challenge is this: Build the tallest free-standing tower possible from a single piece of paper and 30 cm of masking tape.

3. Present the following ground rules:

   - Your group's final tower may only contain those materials (paper and tape) supplied by the teacher.

   - The tower must not be attached at the base to any surface (e.g., desk, floor) and may not lean against any other surface.

   - You will have 30 minutes for official design and construction.

## STANDARDS

**SCIENCE**
Abilities necessary to do
scientific inquiry
Abilities of technological
design

**MATH**
Geometry
Measurement
Problem solving
Reasoning and proof

**SCIENCE**
Understanding about
scientific inquiry
Understanding about
science and technology

- Your tower must stand on its own for 10 seconds or longer.

- The height will be measured from the base to the highest point.

- You can have your tower "officially" measured as many times as possible within the 30-minute time limit; that is, you can keep adding to it as time permits.

4. The following scoring plan pits students only against gravity and eliminates any overt and unnecessary competition between groups:

Over 50 cm = Good

Over 80 cm = Outstanding

Over 100 cm = Spectacular

Over 150 cm = A Masterpiece of Engineering and Design!

5. Tower-building time should be broken into two sections: practice time and official time. Practice time will last for 30 minutes. Student groups receive several pieces of paper, scissors, 30 cm of masking tape, and a meterstick to check their progress. Ask and brainstorm, "What possible shapes or designs could you use?" Students should be encouraged to test as wide a variety of tower designs as possible to find the one with the greatest potential. For younger students, allow more practice time and be willing to help with design ideas.

Keep in mind that air conditioning, open doors, and/or open windows can create breezes that will topple towers and frustrate participants during this activity.

6. Official tower time begins when practice period ends, and lasts for another 30 minutes. Be sure that students surrender any extra paper and tape left over from practice time. You could take a break between the two periods to discuss practice efforts, likely structural candidates, and so on. This discussion would allow students to hypothesize about the tower designs that are most likely to meet the challenge. Or, to encourage separate efforts by the student construction groups, you could dispense with that discussion, moving directly from practice into official time.

7. When official time begins, student groups should receive a single sheet of paper and another 30 cm of tape. To make sure that practice paper is not accidentally incorporated into official towers (thus providing extra construction material), use two different colors of paper, one for practice and one for the official tower. With a list of student groups in hand, circulate and verify student tower height measurements

whenever students ask, documenting their progress on the list. They may continue to add to their towers throughout the time period, so some groups may ask to be officially measured more than once.

8.  Conclude with a classwide discussion and analysis of the activity, including a presentation of each of the towers constructed. Ask students, "What would you do differently next time? What did you enjoy about this activity? What would you like to know about towers?"

## Discussion Questions

Ask students the following:

1.  Which designs worked? Which didn't? How do you explain these results?

2.  What geometric shapes do you see in the completed towers? (Consider the towers in cross section as well as in lateral view.) What other shapes did you experiment with? Why do you suppose that certain shapes work better than others in tower design?

3.  How important were measurements in this activity? Explain your answer.

4.  How did your completed towers compare with the real towers we listed on the chalkboard? How were your towers similar to those? How did they differ?

5.  What sort of training do you think a person would need if he or she wanted to design and build real towers?

## Assessment

Suggestions for specific ways to assess student understanding are provided in parentheses.

1.  Were students actively involved in building and analyzing the design of free-standing paper towers? (Use observations made during Procedures 5–7 as performance assessments, and use responses to Discussion Question 1 as an embedded assessment.)

2.  Were students able to recognize geometric shapes in their tower designs? (Use Discussion Question 2 as embedded evidence or as a prompt for a science journal entry.)

3.  Were students able to measure accurately? (Use observations made during Procedures 5 and 7 as a performance assessment, and use responses to Discussion Question 3 as an embedded assessment.)

4.  Were students able to explain similarities and differences between real towers and their own paper towers? (Use Discussion Question 4 as embedded evidence or as a prompt for a science journal entry.)

**RUBRIC 4.1**
**Sample rubric using these assessment options**

| | Achievement Level | | |
|---|---|---|---|
| | **Developing**<br>**1** | **Proficient**<br>**2** | **Exemplary**<br>**3** |
| Were students actively involved in building and analyzing the design of free-standing paper towers? | Only marginally involved with tower design, construction, and analysis | Appropriately and significantly involved in tower design, construction, and analysis | Took a leadership role in tower design, construction, and analysis |
| Were students able to recognize geometric shapes in their tower designs? | Unsuccessfully attempted to identify geometric shapes in their tower designs | Recognized several geometric shapes in their tower designs | Recognized geometric shapes and could explain their impact on tower design |
| Were students able to measure accurately? | Unsuccessfully attempted to measure tower height | Successfully measured tower height | Successfully measured several aspects of tower design |
| Were students able to explain similarities and differences between real towers and their own paper towers? | Unsuccessfully attempted to explain similarities and differences between real towers and their own to any significant extent | Successfully explained several similarities and differences between real towers and their own | Successfully explained similarities and differences and were also able to explain their implications for tower design and construction |

# Other Options and Extensions

1.  Homework: Ask students to identify towers or towerlike structures in their homes or in the community. As a further extension, students can draw the structures or construct three-dimensional models.

2.  Instruct students to build a paper model of a real tower (e.g., skyscraper, radio tower, Eiffel Tower, Washington Monument, Egyptian obelisk, Leaning Tower of Pisa). This could be done on an individual basis, by cooperative groups, or by the entire class.

3.  Have students conduct research (e.g., library, internet, interviews) into various towers of interest: strange towers, tallest towers, towers in history, most beautiful towers, and so on.

**4.** Rather than building a tall tower, have students design and construct a beautiful tower, a functional tower, an intimidating tower, and/or a fantasy tower.

## Resources

Adams. B. 2006. London Bridge is falling down. *Science and Children* 43 (8): 49–51.

Junior Engineering Technical Society. 1989. Engineering science in the classroom. *Science and Children* 26 (8): 20–23.

Kamii, C. 2006. Measurement of length: How can we teach it better? *Teaching Children Mathematics* 13 (3): 154–158.

Martin, S., J. Sharp, and L. Zachary. 2004. Thinking engineering. *Science and Children* 41 (4): 18–23.

Pace, G., and C. Larsen. 1992. On design technology. *Science and Children* 29 (5): 12–15, 16.

Scarnati, J. 1996. There go the Legos. *Science and Children* 33 (7): 28–30.

Tepper, A. B. 1999. A journey through geometry: Designing a city park. *Teaching Children Mathematics* 5 (6): 348.

Toll, D., and S. Stump. 2007. Characteristics of shapes. *Teaching Children Mathematics* 13 (9): 472–473.

# Activity 5

## Designing and Constructing a Load-Bearing Structure

## Overview

We rely on many structures to bear loads. Examples such as bridges, chairs, shelves, tall buildings, and even our own legs must support weight consistently and effectively. But where do the human-designed examples come from? Who designs these structures and how do they do it? In this activity, students get to apply science and mathematics as they get a hands-on and process-oriented experience of engineering, architecture, and design. First, they explore the properties of wire as a sculptural medium, and then they utilize some of that knowledge as they devise and build a load-bearing structure using nothing but 10 pipe cleaners.

## Processes/Skills

- Observing
- Measuring
- Predicting
- Describing
- Inferring
- Experimenting
- Communicating
- Developing spatial reasoning
- Constructing
- Comparing
- Reflecting
- Recognizing shapes and patterns

- Problem solving
- Analyzing
- Creating
- Designing
- Inquiring
- Applying
- Cooperating

## Recommended For

*Grades 5–8: Small-group instruction*
Adjust for grades 5 and 6 by considering the specific shapes of load-bearing structures in detail during Procedure 2. Examine the question, What sorts of designs are most likely to be successful and why?

## Time Required

1–2 hours

## Materials Required for Main Activity

- Various wiry materials: pipe cleaners (two different colors) and/or actual wire (copper wire, baling wire, galvanized wire, steel wire, thick wire, thin wire, etc.)
- Wire snippers (several pairs)
- Pliers (several pairs)
- Art books with photos of sculptures and/or actual pieces of sculpture
- Photos or illustrations of towers
- Lots of pipe cleaners (at least 15 per student group, of various colors if possible)
- Scissors
- Metric rulers
- Lots of pennies (or other small, standardized weights such as washers or fishing weights)
- Plastic cups
- Balances/scales

# Connecting to the Standards

### NSES
### Grade 5–8 Content Standards:
Standard A: Science as Inquiry

- Abilities necessary to do scientific inquiry (especially thinking critically, using evidence, and applying mathematics)

- Understanding about scientific inquiry (especially emphasizing the value of evidence and mathematics)

Standard E: Science and Technology

- Abilities of technological design (especially identifying, implementing, and evaluating a design solution)

- Understanding about science and technology (especially that science and technology work together, and that technological designs have limitations)

### NCTM
### Standards for Grades 3–8:

- Geometry (especially identifying, naming, comparing, and applying three-dimensional shapes)

- Measurement (especially understanding and applying the metric system)

- Problem Solving (especially applying strategies to solve problems)

- Reasoning and Proof (especially engaging in thinking and reasoning)

# Safety Considerations
Basic classroom safety practices apply. Be certain to instruct students in the proper and safe use of wire snippers, pliers, and scissors before conducting this activity (or simply presnip wire into suitable lengths). In Step 1, thin wire (20 gauge or less) is preferable from a safety standpoint because it is easier to work with and is less likely than thicker wire to have sharp ends when snipped.

# Activity Objectives
In this activity, students

- design and construct their own load-bearing structures out of pipe cleaners; and

- identify and communicate successful and unsuccessful strategies, shapes, designs, and patterns related to the construction of load-bearing structures.

## Main Activity, Step-by-Step Procedures

1. Begin the activity with an open exploration of wire as a medium for sculpting. Offer the students various wiry materials: pipe cleaners (of varied colors, if possible) and/or actual wire (of varied thickness, or gauge). If you do choose to include wire, you can find it in your hardware store in a wide variety of forms: copper wire, baling wire, galvanized wire, steel wire, thick wire, thin wire, and so on. If you use wire, you'll also need some pliers and snippers. Pipe cleaners can be cut with scissors. Thin wire is easier (and therefore safer) to bend, cut, and manipulate. Demonstrate to students that by twisting the wire together it can be formed into nearly any shape. Ask them to use their imaginations to decide what they would like to create. Show some photos of sculptures to stimulate their imaginations. You might ask all students to sit with their eyes closed, take a few calming breaths, and visualize their sculptures. Then let everyone get busy making a boat, a car, a building, an animal, a tree, or whatever they wish. Some might enjoy sculpting their interpretation of an abstract concept (such as "knowledge" or "peace") or a personal feeling. Compare and discuss the projects when completed. Ask students what they liked about sculpting with wire and how they feel about their creations.

2. Ask students, "Can you think of some structures that have to bear weight?" Possible answers might include the wooden frame of a house, a table, the human femur bone, a ladder, a column, the steel girders in a skyscraper, a tree trunk, and so on. Photos and/or illustrations would be helpful here. Students could even draw their own pictures of some of the structures. Generate and record as many responses as possible. Ask, "What characteristics do all these load-bearing structures have in common? How do they differ? What do you notice about their shapes? Are there any ways in which their shapes are similar or different? How does the structure of something that must bear a relatively heavy load differ from that of something that must only support a light load?"

3. Explain to the class that student groups will design and build their own load-bearing structures out of pipe cleaners. The challenge is this: Can each group design and build a structure that will hold a plastic cup containing 50 pennies (or other small weights,

**STANDARDS**

**SCIENCE**
Abilities necessary to do scientific inquiry
Abilities of technological design

**MATH**
Geometry
Measurement
Problem solving
Reasoning and proof

totaling approximately 140 g) at least 10 cm off the table top, using nothing but 10 pipe cleaners? Explain that there will be a classwide competition for the structure that can hold the most pennies at least 10 cm off the table top. The following ground rules should be explained and discussed to make sure that the students understand:

- You may not use any materials other than the pipe cleaners, but you don't have to use all 10 if you don't need them.

- Your structure may not be attached to the table and may not touch or lean against anything but the table.

- The structure must support the cup of 50 pennies for at least 10 seconds, which the referee (the teacher) must time.

- You will have 30 minutes for trial-and-error "design time" and 45 minutes to construct the "official" structure. You'll get 5 "trial-and-error" and 10 "official" pipe cleaners. (It's a good idea to make sure that the two sets of pipe cleaners are different colors to eliminate accidental mixing of extra materials into the official structure.)

4. Each group should receive 5 practice pipe cleaners, a cup with a sealed bag containing pennies, a metric ruler, and a pair of scissors. Give students 30 minutes to plan their structure, encouraging each group to brainstorm together and consider a range of possible designs. An important part of this process will be to consider the geometric aspects of the design possibilities; for instance, what are the advantages of various shapes, including square, rectangle, triangle, or column? Remind students that in a brainstorming session the idea is to generate as many ideas as possible without judging them as good or bad. The final design is then chosen from that list of ideas. Suggest that they sketch potential structural plans on paper before actually building.

5. When the practice time is up, give each group the 10 official pipe cleaners and let them begin creating their final structure. Circulate among groups and offer encouragement, but only offer design suggestions to alleviate especially high frustration levels. Don't offer too much help; this exercise allows students to develop their own means of problem solving, and too much teacher assistance will diminish that process. Test each group's structure for its 50-penny-supporting capability as requested. Be sure that each group has a structure to enter in the classwide competition.

**SCIENCE**
Understanding about scientific inquiry
Understanding about science and technology

6. When the 45-minute time period is up, ask all groups to stop work and to gather around for the competition. Take one structure at a time and test for its ability to support the cup of pennies. Keep adding pennies (in increments of 10) until only one structure remains. How many pennies could it hold before it collapsed? Weigh the pennies to find out how many grams they represent. Engage the class in a discussion of successful and unsuccessful shapes, designs, and patterns. Explore the conclusions that can be drawn about the effective design of load-bearing structures.

7. If time and student interest permit, allow groups to confer as you rechallenge them for a second try at building a strong load-bearing structure. Often the second time around, using the same rules, procedures, and materials, is when many students really "get it."

## Discussion Questions

Ask students the following:

1. Why do load-bearing structures need to be designed carefully?

2. How is mathematics important in designing/engineering load-bearing structures? For instance, what patterns or shapes were useful and how did you identify them?

3. Which load-bearing designs are also aesthetically/artistically pleasing? That is, is art important in designing/engineering load-bearing structures? Why? Under what circumstances would the aesthetic appearance of such a structure become important?

4. What else would you like to know about load-bearing structures? How could you find answers to your questions?

## Assessment

Suggestions for specific ways to assess student understanding are provided in parentheses.

1. Were student groups able to successfully design and construct their own load-bearing structures out of pipe cleaners? (Use observations made during Procedures 3–6 as performance assessments.)

2. Could students identify and communicate about successful and unsuccessful strategies, shapes, designs, and patterns related to construction of load-bearing structures? That is, were they able to draw effective conclusions about designing load-bearing structures? (Use

student responses to Discussion Questions 1–4 as embedded assessments or as writing prompts for science journal entries.)

**RUBRIC 5.1**
**Sample rubric using these assessment options**

| | Achievement Level | | |
| --- | --- | --- | --- |
| | **Developing**<br>**1** | **Proficient**<br>**2** | **Exemplary**<br>**3** |
| Were student groups able to successfully design and construct their own load-bearing structures out of pipe cleaners? | Unsuccessfully attempted to design and construct a load-bearing structure | Successfully designed and constructed a load-bearing structure | Took a leadership role in the successful design of their team's structure |
| Were students able to draw effective conclusions about designing load-bearing structures? | Attempted to draw significant conclusions about structural design, but were unable to do so | Drew several significant conclusions about the design of their own structure | Clearly explained and discussed several significant conclusions about their own and others' structural designs |

# Other Options and Extensions

1. Try different but related challenges: Have students build a structure that elevates the load only to a 5 cm height and determine how the maximum weight supported compares with that of the 10 cm version. Then students should build a structure that elevates the load to a 15 cm height and do the same comparison. Instruct students to graph "height" versus "maximum weight supported" and look for a relationship between these two variables.

2. Homework: Ask students to make a list of load-supporting structures found in their home, neighborhood, and community.

3. Explore ways to make more wire sculptures. Students should consider making wire mobiles and/or creating sculptures that go along with a favorite book or story. Also encourage students to try making geometric/arithmetic sculptures (e.g., all triangles, or using squares of increasing sizes).

## Resources
Adams, B. 2006. London Bridge is falling down. *Science and Children* 43 (8): 49–51.
Anderson, J. 1972. Aestheometry…Constructions in space mathematics. *Science and Children* 10 (1): 31–32.

Junior Engineering Technical Society. 1989. Engineering science in the class-room. *Science and Children* 26 (8): 20–23.

Kajander, A. E. 1999. Creating opportunities for children to think math-ematically. *Teaching Children Mathematics* 5: 480–486.

Martin, S., J. Sharp, and L. Zachary. 2004. Thinking engineering. *Science and Children* 41 (4): 18–23.

Pace, G., and C. Larsen. On design technology. *Science and Children* 29 (5): 12–15, 16.

Scarnati, J. 1996. There go the Legos. *Science and Children* 33 (7): 28–30.

Toll, D., and S. Stump. 2007. Characteristics of shapes. *Teaching Children Mathematics* 13 (9): 472–473.

# + Physical Science

## Activity 6

### Investigating the Pinhole Camera and Camera Obscura

## Overview

In this activity, students explore the nature of light, including the fact that it travels in straight lines, by building and using two visual tools. The first is a simple pinhole camera—a box with a pinhole opening. The second is a camera obscura—a tool of historical interest, particularly in the arts. The camera obscura, basically a pinhole camera with a lens, was a forerunner of the modern camera and allowed 17th- and 18th-century artists to make very accurate sketches of their subjects. During the activity, students will explore the operation of these simple instruments and will learn why, historically, the camera obscura was an important tool for many artists. The entire lesson will also serve as an introduction to the art of photography, which will be explored more fully in Activity 7.

## Processes/Skills

- Observing
- Constructing
- Measuring
- Graphing
- Predicting
- Describing
- Inferring
- Designing experiments
- Comparing
- Creating
- Sketching

- Appreciating
- Cooperating
- Communicating

## Recommended For

*Grades 5–8: Small-group instruction*

This activity can be adapted for grades 5 and 6 by prebuilding the shoe-box cameras in Procedure 2, toning down or eliminating the graphs in Procedure 3, and demonstrating a prebuilt camera obscura rather than having students do the building and exploring as in Procedures 6 and 7.

## Time Required

2–4 hours

## Materials Required for Main Activity

- Shoe boxes
- Pin or needle
- Transparent tape
- Paper
- Scissors
- Flashlights
- Metersticks
- Graph paper
- Hand lenses
- Medium-sized cardboard box(es)
- Large appliance box(es)
- Pencils/charcoal/crayons

## Optional Materials

- Small mirrors (metal or plastic, not glass)
- Dark cloth for camera obscura shrouding

# Materials Required for Going Further

- A variety of drawing and painting materials
- Paper
- Lens for camera obscura
- Variety of materials to build focusing tube (e.g., cardboard tubes, cardboard, masking tape)

# Connecting to the Standards

### NSES
### Grade 5–8 Content Standards:
Standard A: Science as Inquiry

- Abilities necessary to do scientific inquiry (especially about systematic observation using appropriate tools and techniques, including mathematics)
- Understanding about scientific inquiry (especially about the importance of mathematics in scientific inquiry)

Standard B: Physical Science

- Transfer of energy (especially regarding the interaction of light with matter)

Standard F: Science in Personal and Social Perspectives

- Science and technology in society (especially how technology influences society)

### NCTM
### Standards for Grades 3–8:

- Measurement (especially understanding and applying the metric system)
- Data Analysis and Probability (especially displaying relevant data to answer questions)
- Communication (especially communicating their mathematical thinking clearly)

# Safety Considerations
Basic classroom safety practices apply. Be sure that students understand the dangers associated with staring at any bright light source, particularly the

## INVESTIGATING THE PINHOLE CAMERA AND CAMERA OBSCURA

Sun, and that they protect their eyes at all times. Only the teacher should handle the needle or pin used to make the pinhole in the shoe-box camera and the camera obscura. Be sure that students know how to behave safely in the darkened room.

## Activity Objectives

In this activity, students

- construct and operate the pinhole camera and the camera obscura;

- explain how they know that light travels in straight lines;

- quantify and explain the relationship between the distance from the light source and the size of the image seen, using the pinhole camera; and

- understand the historical place of the camera obscura.

## Background Information

The camera obscura ("dark chamber") was a forerunner of the modern camera and was used by many great 17th- and 18th-century painters, including Jan Vermeer and Paul Sandby, as an aid in making accurate preliminary drawings. It was essentially a modified pinhole camera, a box fitted with lens and mirror that projected the chosen image onto a piece of paper placed on the base of the box. One side of the box was kept open, allowing access to the paper, and the whole device was covered with a curtain. The artist, shrouded by the curtain, could then easily trace the image that was projected on the paper in the box.

## Main Activity, Step-by-Step Procedures

1.  Ask students to brainstorm in response to the question, "What do your eyes, a cardboard box, and a camera all have in common?" Encourage a variety of answers.

2.  Have students build a very simple pinhole camera (*camera* is from Latin for "room or chamber") using a shoe box. Be sure that you've built your own ahead of time so that you have a feel for the camera's construction and operation. Have students cut out one end of the box and replace it with a piece of plain white paper. Then they make the pinhole very small in the center of the other end of the box (see Figure 6.1). Finally they cut a small triangle (equilateral, about 3 cm per side) from the discarded end of the shoe box and secure it with transparent tape to the center

**SCIENCE**
Abilities necessary to do scientific inquiry

of a flashlight lens, as in Figure 6.2. Darken the room and have each group of students shine the light at the pinhole in their camera. This might be easier if the box is held and "adjusted" while the light remains stationary. What image appears on the box's "screen"? Have students explore the properties of this apparatus, and then ask them to share what they have discovered and what they would like to know about this camera. Point out that the triangle is projected through the pinhole because light travels in straight lines, and the light is absorbed by the triangular piece of cardboard. Ask, "How is this camera similar to other cameras you have seen? How is it different?"

**FIGURE 6.1. Pinhole camera**

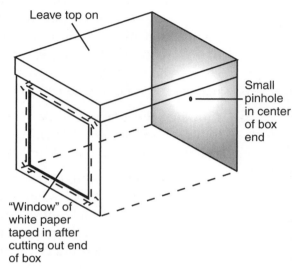

Leave top on

Small pinhole in center of box end

"Window" of white paper taped in after cutting out end of box

**FIGURE 6.2. Flashlight with cardboard triangle taped to lens**

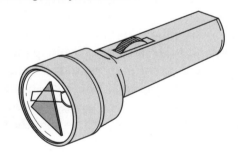

**MATH**
Measurement
Data analysis and
 probability
Communication

3. Using the same pinhole and flashlight arrangement, tell the students that their job is to find out what relationship exists between the camera's distance from the light source and the size of the image seen. Have them hypothesize what they think will happen to the size of the image as the box is moved farther from the light. Then they can collect data by measuring the image size at various distances from the light and record their findings on Activity Sheet 6.1, p. 67. Students can make the data into a line graph (independent variable, i.e., distance, on *x* axis; and dependent variable, i.e., image size, on *y* axis), and each student or group can explain in writing what the graph shows (i.e., the relationship between the two variables).

## STANDARDS

**SCIENCE**
Science and technology in
society

4. Ask students, "How might an artist use a camera such as the one you made? How could he or she modify the pinhole camera to be useful in sketching an accurate picture?" Allow time for groups to ponder the question and perhaps make illustrations to explain their proposed modifications. Encourage a variety of answers from groups/individuals, recalling that this is an opportunity for all to engage their imaginations and is not the time to judge or criticize responses.

5. Introduce the history and use of the camera obscura. Show, examine, and discuss examples of Vermeer's paintings. Notice his careful attention to detail, made possible in large part by the camera obscura.

   You'll definitely want to make and operate a camera obscura of your own before asking students to try this. Making the camera is easy, but it may take a bit of creative "play" to obtain clear images. Remember that the pinhole must be very small and that both instruments work best under very dark conditions. This activity is definitely an adventure in trial and error.

6. Have students construct a camera obscura, using one of several pinhole-type designs. The simplest design is nothing more than a box camera arrangement that a student can put his or her head into, thus allowing the student to see the image (see Figure 6.3). Use a medium-sized box, and instead of the "screen" at the far end of the chamber, just tape a piece of white paper on the inside of the box. The image comes through the pinhole and falls on the paper. Try varying the size of the pinhole. The user's head enters from the bottom of the box. Be sure to block any extra light from entering from below by stuffing/shrouding the area around the shoulders with a blanket.

   Another possibility is to make the camera obscura so large that students can climb completely inside. This can be done by turning an empty appliance box into an oversized pinhole camera, cutting a door in the side for access (see Figure 6.4). Once inside, it is easy for students to draw the image that falls on the taped-up "screen" of white paper.

   These designs may be improved by adding one or more components to the camera obscura, such as adjusting the image with a lens, reflecting the image with a mirror, and/or opening the side of the chamber and adding shrouding to keep out unwanted light. Let students explore different ways of modifying the apparatus. The camera obscura will operate best in bright light, especially in sunlight.

7. Allow each student to make a sketch using a camera obscura. Then have students sketch the same image, without using the apparatus.

Ask them how the two drawings compare. Introduce the concepts of *accuracy* (conformity to truth or to a standard or model; exactness) and *precision* (the degree of refinement with which an operation is performed or a measurement stated). That is, *accuracy* refers to the sketch's nearness to the actual view, whereas *precision* refers to the similarity of repeat sketches of the same view. Ask students, "What does it mean to make accurate drawings, and how does the camera obscura help? Are all painters interested in accuracy? Under what circumstances would mathematicians or scientists need to be accurate or make accurate drawings?" Students could be asked to explore these questions (and/ or others) in a journal writing assignment. Find out what questions students have about the camera obscura or pinhole camera, and what further investigations they would like to undertake.

**FIGURE 6.3. Small camera obscura**

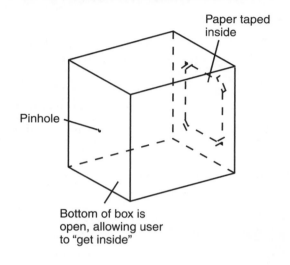

Paper taped inside

Pinhole

Bottom of box is open, allowing user to "get inside"

**FIGURE 6.4. Large camera obscura**

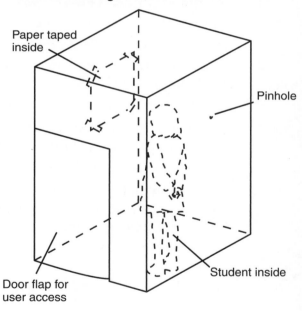

Paper taped inside

Pinhole

Door flap for user access

Student inside

## Discussion Questions

Ask students the following:

1. What did you enjoy about making and/or using the pinhole camera? The camera obscura?

2. As you performed these investigations, what did you learn about light? What else would you like to know?

3. Under what circumstances would a camera obscura be a useful tool for an artist?

4. How do the pinhole camera and camera obscura differ from a modern camera?

## Assessment

Suggestions for specific ways to assess student understanding are provided in parentheses.

1. Did students successfully construct and operate the pinhole camera and camera obscura? (Use observations made during Procedures 2, 3, 6, and 7 as performance assessments.)

2. Were students able to explain how they know that light travels in straight lines? (Use Discussion Question 2 as an embedded assessment or as a writing prompt for a science journal entry.)

3. Did students effectively use the pinhole camera to graphically portray the relationship between the distance from the light source and the size of the image seen? (Use Procedure 3 as a performance assessment.)

4. Were students able to explain the value of the camera obscura to painters, and to see the instrument in historical perspective? (Use Discussion Questions 3 and 4 as embedded assessments or as writing prompts for science journal entries.)

## RUBRIC 6.1
### Sample rubric using these assessment options

| | Achievement Level | | |
| --- | --- | --- | --- |
| | Developing 1 | Proficient 2 | Exemplary 3 |
| Did students successfully construct and operate the pinhole camera and camera obscura? | Attempted to construct and operate the cameras but were unsuccessful | Successfully constructed and operated the cameras | Successfully constructed and operated the cameras and were able to explain how they operated |
| Were students able to explain how they know that light travels in straight lines? | Attempted unsuccessfully to explain | Successfully explained based on their experiences with the cameras | Successfully explained based on their experiences with the cameras and added other examples, such as shadows |
| Did students effectively use the pinhole camera to graphically portray the relationship between the distance from the light source and the size of the image seen? | Attempted but were unsuccessful at graphing the data or explaining the relationship between the variables | Successfully graphed the data and were able to explain the relationship between the variables | Successfully graphed the data, were able to explain the relationship between the variables, and could make accurate predictions about distance and image size using the graph |
| Were students able to explain the value of the camera obscura to painters, and to see the instrument in historical perspective? | Attempted unsuccessfully to explain | Successfully explained, at a basic level, the value of the camera in historical perspective | Successfully explained, in detail (including the use of examples), the value of the camera in historical perspective |

# Going Further

Students can elaborate on their camera obscura sketches using materials of their choice (such as paint, charcoal, crayons, pastels, and collage). Ask the individual student artists, "What do you like about your own pictures? What aspects would you change? Why?" Hang the finished products, with student approval. (Don't hang a picture if the artist doesn't approve.) Encourage a discussion of similarities and differences, especially in regard to the instrument-enhanced perspectives of students' work. For example, you might ask, "How might these depictions differ if you hadn't used the camera obscura?"

# Other Options and Extensions

1.  Introduce and encourage student research into the structure and function of the vertebrate eye (see Activities 16 and 17 for more on this topic). Outside reading, diagrams, and illustrations would be

appropriate. Consider dissecting cow or sheep eyes to provide a hands-on experience.

2. Lead the class in using the large camera obscura under a variety of lighting conditions to determine its strengths and limitations. Encourage student suggestions regarding relevant modifications in its design.

3. To get a brighter, clearer image, try building a camera obscura that uses a simple lens rather than a pinhole. An appropriate lens may be purchased at *www.anchoroptics.com*; consider the grade positive meniscus lens, which will be reusable for years. Challenge the students to design a focusing mount for the lens using cardboard tubing, masking tape, and/or other supplies.

## Resources

Gore, G. 1974. Pinhole photography for young students. *Science and Children* 12 (1): 14–16.

McMahon, M. 2002. Picture this. *Science and Children* 39 (7): 42–45.

McQueen, R. 1996. Pinhole. *Photo Instructor* 18: 9–10.

Millward, R. E. 2000. Photographing wildlife. *Science and Children* 37 (5): 28–31, 53.

Robertson, B. 2007. When drawing graphs from collected data, why don't you just connect the dots? *Science and Children* 45 (2): 56–59.

Rommel-Esham, K. 2005. Do you see what I see? *Science and Children* 43 (1): 40–43.

Smith, L. 1985. *The visionary pinhole*. Salt Lake City, UT: Peregrine Smith.

Victor, R. 1984. The return of the sun dragon. *Science and Children* 21 (8): 16–18.

Whitin, D. J., and P. Whitin. 2003. Talk counts: Discussing graphs with young children. *Teaching Children Mathematics* 10 (3): 142–149.

Worne, J. 1984. Pinhole photography—A budget saver. *School Arts* 83 (6): 19–22.

## ACTIVITY SHEET 6.1
### Investigating the Pinhole Camera and Camera Obscura

What do you think will happen to the size of the image as the camera is moved farther away from the light source? Explain your answer.

Collect data by measuring the image size at various distances from the light. Record your data in the table below.

| Distance From Light Source to Camera | Size of Image |
| --- | --- |
|  |  |
|  |  |
|  |  |
|  |  |
|  |  |

What conclusions can you reach, based on your data?

# +Physical Science

# Activity 7

## Recording Images Using a Simple Pinhole Camera

## Overview

In this lesson, students develop and expand their observational skills and technological understanding by building and operating a pinhole camera. The interdisciplinary connections are in the realm of application in this motivating activity. The lesson provides students with opportunities to connect technology (the camera itself) to its aesthetic product (the photograph).

## Processes/Skills

- Observing
- Constructing
- Measuring
- Creating
- Comparing
- Imagining
- Recognizing shapes
- Predicting
- Inferring
- Analyzing
- Appreciating
- Problem solving
- Cooperating
- Communicating

## Recommended For

*Grades 5–8: Small-group instruction*
You can adapt the activity for grades 5 and 6 by pre-assembling the pinhole cameras or by using the premade cameras discussed in Procedure 7. You'll almost certainly want to load the photosensitive papers into the cameras yourself for younger students.

## Time Required

2–4 hours

## Materials Required for Main Activity

- Black cardboard
- Inexpensive photography paper or sun paper (These materials should be available from a local photography store, a photography supply catalog, or a website such as *www.freestylephoto.biz*.)
- Masking tape
- Scissors
- 15- to 25-watt red lightbulb and lamp (These materials should be available from a local photography store, a photography supply catalog, or a website such as *www.freestylephoto.biz*.)

## Connecting to the Standards

### NSES
**Grade 5–8 Content Standards:**
Standard A: Science as Inquiry

- Abilities necessary to do scientific inquiry (especially about systematic observation using appropriate tools and techniques, including mathematics)

Standard B: Physical Science

- Transfer of energy (especially regarding the interaction of light with matter)

Standard E: Science and Technology

- Abilities of technological design (especially evaluating the suitability of completed technological products)

- Understanding about science and technology (especially that science and technology work together, and that technological designs have limitations)

Standard F: Science in Personal and Social Perspectives

- Science and technology in society (especially how technology influences society)

## NCTM
### Standards for Grades 3–8:

- Geometry (especially applying three-dimensional shapes)

- Measurement (especially understanding and applying the metric system)

- Problem Solving (especially applying strategies to solve problems)

- Communication (especially communicating their mathematical thinking clearly)

## Safety Considerations
Basic classroom safety practices apply. Be sure that students understand the dangers associated with staring at any bright light source, particularly the Sun, and that they protect their eyes at all times. If students intend to photograph one another, be sure to first obtain parental consent.

## Activity Objectives
In this activity, students

- construct and operate pinhole cameras;

- understand and explain the fundamentals of camera construction, including the importance of exposure time; and

- compare photography to the other visual arts, including painting, drawing, and sculpting.

## Background Information
The pinhole camera has no lens and a very small opening for light (aperture). The shutter (the device that allows light to pass through the aperture) is operated manually. The smaller the aperture, the greater the resolution (sharpness) of the resulting photographs. Pinhole photographs are made by allowing light to enter the aperture and strike plastic or paper containing light-sensitive chemicals (film), seated within the camera. A chemical process (film developing) applied to the film then makes the image visible (photograph).

# Main Activity, Step-by-Step Procedures

1. Ask students, "How are the pinhole camera and camera obscura from Activity 6 like a modern camera? How are they different from a modern camera?" (If you haven't done Activity 6, you could demonstrate the basic function of a simple pinhole camera to the class.) A diagram and a camera would be useful as visual aids at this point. Ask, "How would you modify a pinhole camera so that it could record an image itself?" Encourage a variety of responses, possibly having students illustrate their ideas with simple diagrams.

2. Have each group construct a pinhole camera similar to the one used in Activity 6, with several important modifications: (a) instead of using a shoe box, the cube-shaped chamber will be constructed from pieces of black cardboard, as in Figure 7.1, and (b) instead of cutting a "window" of white paper in the end of the chamber, students will secure a piece of photosensitive paper (either sun paper or inexpensive photography paper) to the inside of the end of the box (see Figure 7.2). The camera can be constructed under normal lighting conditions, but the photosensitive paper will have to be inserted under darkroom conditions. (If you use sun paper, you will only need a well-darkened room.) These conditions can be accomplished by simply taping the paper in place by feel over the entire inside of the box-end in a completely darkened room, or by using a 15- to 25-watt red lightbulb in an otherwise completely darkened room (such as a small, windowless storage room with the base of the door covered). Under darkroom conditions, after securing the photosensitive paper, place a piece of tape over the camera's pinhole to block light from coming in. That piece of tape will be removed when students are ready to record an image.

3. Discuss with the class what makes an interesting photographic image. Exposure to exemplary photographs and/or books of photography will facilitate student analysis, discussion, and creativity in evaluating photo aesthetics. With the photosensitive paper secured and all camera openings thoroughly sealed (including the pinhole), student groups may find an image outside the classroom that they would like to expose and record. A sunny, bright day is ideal for this activity. Because the camera must be motionless during the exposure, students may want to tape the chamber to a chair or stool in preparation for recording the image. Students should aim the camera at the desired image, carefully remove the tape from the pinhole, and expose the photosensitive paper (4–10 seconds for photography paper in direct sunlight, or at least a minute for

**FIGURE 7.1. Construction of pinhole camera**

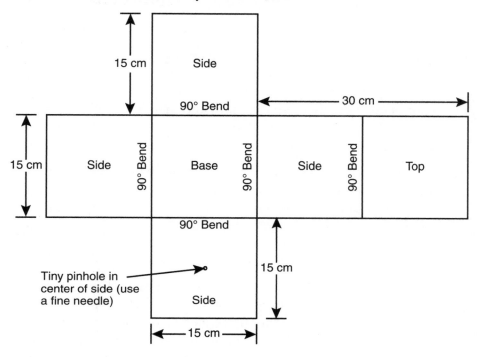

sun paper). A group member should keep track of exposure time, and when the exposure is complete, the pinhole tape seal is gently replaced. Cameras should be marked with members' names to facilitate their return to the correct group. The recorded image should be described briefly in writing, including the exposure time and the general environmental conditions under which the photo was made. (Students can tape the description to the side of the camera.)

**FIGURE 7.2. Completed pinhole camera**

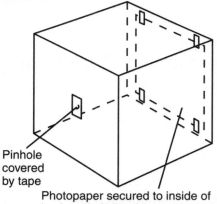

Pinhole covered by tape

Photopaper secured to inside of back wall of chamber — top and pinhole have been sealed with tape

**4.** If you used photography paper, you will need to have the exposures developed. Due to safety concerns, students shouldn't be directly involved in this process unless your experience in photo developing is substantial (and, of course, safety must always be a primary consideration).

5.  When students receive their developed photos, have student groups meet to appreciate and analyze their work. Display photos (with student permission) gallery-style. Invite supportive and aesthetic comments. Initially in small groups and then in whole-class discussion, compare the products of photography to those of other visual arts (such as painting, sculpture, and drawing).

6.  If time permits, a second attempt at recording images will be worthwhile after students have observed, analyzed, compared, and problem solved. For instance, they may want to see what happens if they place the camera in a stationary position (e.g., on a chair) instead of holding it by hand during exposure. Let students try the process again, encouraging imaginative modifications in the exposure stage.

7.  Here is an alternative to constructing the pinhole camera from scratch: Obtain several inexpensive cameras (a local photo shop may donate these if they are persuaded to see the potential benefits involved with cultivating student interest in this area). Remove the shutter/aperture from each camera and attach (with tape) a piece of black cardboard with a tiny pinhole. Using this method, students can make pinhole photos using normal rolls of film. Problems with developing these images are eliminated because they can be processed anywhere.

## Discussion Questions

Ask students the following:

1.  What did you expect your group's recorded image—that is, the photograph—to look like? How did it differ from your expectations?

2.  How would you do this activity differently if you were to do it again?

3.  What problems did you encounter (especially if the image did not turn out quite the way you expected or wanted)? How could you solve those problems?

4.  How is photography like drawing? Like painting? Like sculpture? How is it different? Which do you prefer? Why?

5.  What skills, talents, and/or characteristics do you have that make you a good photographer? Explain.

6. Why is math important in photography? Why is science important in photography?

# Assessment

Suggestions for specific ways to assess student understanding are provided in parentheses.

1. Were students able to successfully construct the cameras? (Use observations made during Procedure 2 as a performance assessment.)

2. Were students able to record images with their pinhole cameras? (Use observations made during Procedures 3, 5, and 6 as performance assessments.)

3. Could students explain the fundamentals of camera construction and operation, including the importance of exposure time? (Use Discussion Questions 1, 2, 3, and 6 as embedded assessments or as writing prompts for science journal entries.)

4. Were students able to compare photography with other arts, such as drawing, sculpting, or painting? (Use Discussion Questions 4 and 5 as embedded assessments or as writing prompts for science journal entries.)

## RUBRIC 7.1
### Sample rubric using these assessment options

| | Achievement Level | | |
| --- | --- | --- | --- |
| | Developing 1 | Proficient 2 | Exemplary 3 |
| Were students able to successfully construct the cameras? | Attempted to construct a camera, but were unsuccessful | Successfully constructed a camera | Took a leadership role in successfully constructing a camera |
| Were students able to record images with their pinhole cameras? | Attempted to record an image, but were unsuccessful | Successfully recorded images with the camera | Took a leadership role in successfully recording images |
| Could students explain the fundamentals of camera construction and operation, including the importance of exposure time? | Attempted to explain, but were not successful to any significant extent | Successfully explained the fundamentals of camera construction and operation | Explained the fundamentals of camera construction and operation in detail, including exposure time, using examples |
| Were students able to compare photography with other arts, such as drawing, sculpting, or painting? | Attempted to compare photography to other arts, but were not successful to any significant extent | Successfully compared photography to other arts | Compared photography to other arts in detail, including examples |

# Other Options and Extensions

1. Homework: Encourage students to use a pinhole camera to take more photos at home with family members. They can make a collection of favorite family pinhole photos.

2. Encourage students to study photographs, old and new. Have students bring photos into class to share, and ask them to discuss the setting, the equipment and techniques used (if known), and the effect on the viewer.

3. Encourage students to study the history of photography and famous photographers such as Anne Brigman and Alfred Stieglitz.

4. Have students compare the function of the modern camera to the function of the eye (see Activities 6, 16, and 17). They should pay particular attention to the retina/film analogy.

5. Have students use the internet to research the chemistry of the film development process.

## Resources

Gore, G. 1974. Pinhole photography for young students. *Science and Children* 12 (1): 14–16.

Junger, T. 1971. The pinhole camera. *School Arts* 7 (4): 14–15.

McMahon, M. 2002. Picture this. *Science and Children* 39 (7): 42–45.

McQueen, R. 1996. Pinhole. *Photo Instructor* 18: 9–10.

Rommel-Esham, K. 2005. Do you see what I see? *Science and Children* 43 (1): 40–43.

Shull, J. 1974. The hole thing: *A manual of pinhole fotografy.* Dobbs Ferry, NY: Morgan and Morgan.

Smith, L. 1985. *The visionary pinhole.* Salt Lake City, UT: Peregrine Smith.

Toll, D., and S. Stump. 2007. Characteristics of shapes. *Teaching Children Mathematics* 13 (9): 472–473.

Turner, E. E., D. L. Junk, and S. B. Empson. 2007. The power of paper-folding tasks. *Teaching Children Mathematics* 13 (6): 322–329.

Victor, R. 1984. The return of the sun dragon. *Science and Children* 21 (8): 16–18.

Worne, J. 1984. Pinhole photography—A budget saver. *School Arts* 83 (6): 19–22.

# + Physical Science

## Activity 8
### Learning About Levers

## Overview

We see, use, and enjoy levers daily—in the operation of pliers, the action of a seesaw, or the beauty of an Alexander Calder mobile. In fact, parts of the human body are levers; think of the knee, elbow, and other joints as fulcrums, and the long bones as levers. In this activity, student groups will expand their understanding of levers and balance by discovering how weight and fulcrum placement affect lever performance. As a connecting activity, the students will apply what they learn about levers to the creation of dynamic science- or mathematics-related mobiles.

## Processes/Skills

- Observing
- Measuring
- Describing
- Comparing
- Designing investigations
- Communicating
- Inferring
- Analyzing
- Collecting data
- Drawing conclusions from data
- Problem solving
- Recognizing patterns
- Appreciating
- Cooperating

- Applying
- Creating
- Reflecting
- Enjoying

## Recommended For

*Grades 5–8: Small-group instruction*

For fifth graders, you can preconstruct the cardboard fulcrums and consider taping the small weights to the meterstick in Procedure 2 to make balancing a bit easier. Perhaps perform Procedure 5 as a demonstration rather than as a hands-on activity. Be sure to offer assistance to younger students when it comes to the Activity Sheet inquiry and analysis; you could even do that part of the investigation as a whole class.

## Time Required

1–3 hours

## Materials Required for Main Activity

- Metersticks
- Cardboard fulcrums (see Figure 8.1, p. 82)
- Any sort of small, uniformly shaped weights (coins, gram weights, fishing weights, etc.)
- Masking tape
- Cord, string, and/or fishing line
- Lightweight levers for the mobile (drinking straws, bamboo shishkabob skewers, dowels, sticks or branches, sturdy wire such as cut-up clothes hangers, etc.)
- A variety of materials to act as weights in the mobile (cardboard cutouts, shells, leaves, feathers, aluminum foil shapes, old electronic components, etc.)
- Various art materials for mobile (paint, paste or glue, etc.)

# Connecting to the Standards

### NSES
### Grade 5–8 Content Standards:
Standard A: Science as Inquiry

- Abilities necessary to do scientific inquiry (especially observing carefully, thinking critically about evidence to develop and communicate good explanations, and using mathematics effectively)

- Understandings about scientific inquiry (especially recognizing the importance of mathematics in science and noticing that scientific explanations emphasize evidence and logically consistent arguments)

Standard B: Physical Science

- Motions and forces (especially investigating the effects of balanced and unbalanced forces on an object)

### NCTM
### Standards for Grades 3–8:

- Algebra (especially understanding patterns and relationships)
- Measurement (especially understanding and applying the metric system)
- Problem Solving (especially applying strategies to solve problems)
- Reasoning and Proof (especially engaging in thinking and reasoning)
- Connections (especially recognizing the connections among mathematical ideas and to investigations outside mathematics)

# Safety Considerations
Basic classroom safety practices apply.

# Activity Objectives
In this activity, students

- balance their levers in different ways and explain their techniques;

- deepen their understanding of levers and balance, including identification of the fulcrum, and identify levers in the classroom and in their lives;

- determine the mathematical relationship between the location of the fulcrum and the distance the weight must be placed from the fulcrum to make the lever balance; and

- use the lever concept to build creative science/math mobiles.

**LEARNING ABOUT LEVERS**

# Main Activity, Step-by-Step Procedures

1. Demonstrate the following for the class: Balance a meterstick on your horizontally held index finger. In this case, your finger (acting as the *fulcrum*, or balance point) will be at the 50 cm mark. You could also use a cardboard fulcrum: a piece of sturdy cardboard bent and taped into a "tent" or wedge shape (see Figure 8.1) and placed on a desk or table. Ask students, "What will happen to this 'system' if I move my finger (or the cardboard fulcrum) to the 40 cm mark?" Entertain hypotheses, and then demonstrate the result. Ask students, working in small groups, to explain why the stick didn't fall when the fulcrum was at 50 cm, but it did when the fulcrum was shifted to the 40 cm mark. The responses will probably include the notions that in the first case the stick was balanced, but it was unbalanced in the second case.

**FIGURE 8.1. Fulcrum**

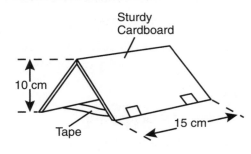

Ask, "What do you mean by *balanced*?" Students should clarify their thinking on this point. Point out that a balanced system can be said to be at *equilibrium*. Inform students that the meterstick is acting as a lever. Ask, "Where else do we find levers?" (seesaw, pry bar, catapult, long bones of the body, scales, etc.).

2. Next, give each student group a set of weights, a meterstick, and a cardboard fulcrum. Ask them to balance the stick on the fulcrum. Now, *without changing the balance point* of the stick (that is, keeping the 50 cm mark at the fulcrum) ask them to tape a small weight (e.g., five pennies, five grams, one fishing weight) on top of one end of the meterstick (see Figure 8.2). Does the stick balance? (No.) Ask, "What can you do to make the stick balance again, *without moving the weight?*" Let the student groups puzzle over this and come up with their own solutions to the problem. You might mention that although they can't move or remove the weights, they can move the stick and they can add weights to the stick. Challenge students to devise as many solutions as they can, try them, and record (in words, drawings, and numbers) their ideas under Step 1 on Activity Sheet 8.1, p. 88. Pose the following questions to students: "What worked and what didn't? What did you think would work

### SCIENCE
Motions and forces

### MATH
Measurement
Problem solving

### SCIENCE
Abilities necessary to do
  scientific inquiry

### MATH
Algebra

that didn't and why didn't it?
What patterns do you see in
the successful solutions?" (The
obvious solution may be to
simply place an equal weight
at the other end of the lever.
But how was balance main-
tained if the balance point was
changed, or if more weight was added to the original end of the
lever?) "What did you discover about levers and balance?"

**FIGURE 8.2. Unbalanced lever**

50 cm

Weight(s)

Taping down
the weight(s)
will help

3. Remove all weights from the lever and move the fulcrum to the
45 cm mark. Does the lever balance? (No.) Challenge the student
groups to find as many ways as possible to make the lever balance,
without moving the fulcrum from the 45 cm mark. Try using only
one weight, then two weights, then three weights. Again, students
must keep a written record of their attempts (see Activity Sheet 8.1,
Step 2), whether successful or not. After allowing sufficient time for
exploration, discuss and analyze the results as a group. Ask students,
"What worked? What didn't? Why or why not? What combinations
of weights did you try? Do you notice any patterns? What have
you learned about levers? What more do you want to know about
levers?"

4. The next step in this investigation is to collect numerical data
about how the lever operates. Using Figure 8.3 as a guide, have
student groups determine the relationship between the location of
the fulcrum and the distance the weight must be placed from the
fulcrum to make the lever balance. Using the metersticks and a
single weight, students should start with the fulcrum at the 45 cm
point on the meterstick and determine the distance from the fulcrum to the weight to make the lever balance. (The weight will vary
depending on the sort of meterstick and the type of weights being
used; experiment here, and then use the same weight throughout
the procedure.) Students should record that distance in Step 3 on
Activity Sheet 8.1. Next, students should move the fulcrum to the
40 cm mark and again determine and record the distance from
fulcrum to weight when balanced. Have them repeat this step,
moving the fulcrum to the 35, 30, 25, and 20 cm marks, each time
recording the weight's distance from the fulcrum when balanced.
Ask students, "What do the results tell you about levers? Based on
your research, please complete the following statement: To balance

**SCIENCE**
Understanding about
scientific inquiry

**MATH**
Reasoning and proof

**MATH**
Connections

the lever as the fulcrum is moved farther from the center, the weight must _____."

**FIGURE 8.3. Distance from fulcrum**

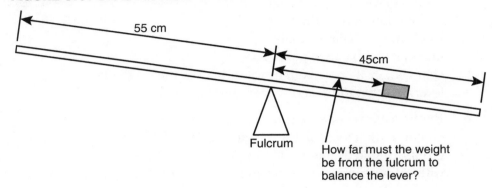

55 cm

45cm

Fulcrum

How far must the weight be from the fulcrum to balance the lever?

5. For the next portion of the lesson each student group will need to have access to a dangling piece of cord. This can be accomplished by running several horizontal "clotheslines" for support at a 5 or 6 ft. height across the classroom and hanging the cords from those—or use whatever means available (e.g., taped or tied to top of a doorway or to the ceiling). Direct the groups to then tie that string to the middle of a lightweight horizontal beam (e.g., drinking straw, sturdy wire, small diameter dowel, bamboo shish-kabob skewer, etc.) so that it hangs evenly. Ask the students if this balancing horizontal beam reminds them of anything. That horizontal piece is actually a lever, although it is "upside down" compared to the earlier levers the students have seen in this activity. The string by which it hangs is the fulcrum. Next, have students tie or tape a short string to each of two small but unequal weights (e.g., a penny and a nickel), and tie the other end of each string to either end of the horizontal lever. By sliding the weights on the lever, they can try to balance it again. Ask students, "How is this lever like the levers used earlier? How is it different? How were you able to make it balance?"

6. Have students use the "upside down" lever idea (see Procedure 5) to construct their own mobiles. Pick a science or mathematics theme (such as geometry, repeating number patterns, found objects from nature, planets, atomic structure, rain, organs of the body, electronics, endangered species, or plant anatomy). Get some sticks, wires, driftwood, or other "lever" crosspieces and some string or fishing

line. Also, students can help to compile objects related to their topic, such as shapes cut out of cardboard, photos pasted onto cardboard or other substances, shells, feathers, leaves, yarn bubbles (saturate yarn with paste, wrap it around a small balloon, allow yarn to dry, pop and remove balloon), crumpled aluminum foil, toothpick sculptures, papier-mâché shapes, or electronic components taken from that broken phone answering machine you've been meaning to throw away. The sky is the limit. Students should tie the objects onto each end of the levers, balancing each lever by moving the "weights" closer to or farther from the fulcrum (i.e., the supporting string). Older students with well-developed motor skills should try to make at least a three- or four-layer mobile (see Figure 8.4). For younger students, two or three layers will suffice. Encourage imagination. Consider making the levers of different lengths, tying another lever onto one end of a lever, or tying more than two objects onto a single lever. After these experiments, ask students, "Does the mobile lever have to be perfectly straight or could it be a curved wire? What other shapes would work? Does the lever have to be perfectly horizontal? How else could it be oriented?" Allow students or student groups to explain their mobiles to the class.

**FIGURE 8.4. Four-layer mobile**

## Discussion Questions

Ask students the following:

1. What is meant by *balance*? How were you able to make your lever balance? What have you discovered about levers?

2. As the fulcrum is moved farther from the center of the lever, what happens to the distance that a weight must be placed in order to keep the lever balanced? How do you know?

3. What does a mobile have to do with levers?

4. Why do you think the object is called a *mobile*?

## Assessment

Suggestions for specific ways to assess student understanding are provided in parentheses.

1. Were students able to balance their levers in different ways and explain their techniques? (Use observations made during Procedures 2–4 as performance assessments.)

2. Were students able to explain how the lever and fulcrum interact and how balance is achieved? (Use Discussion Questions 1–3 as embedded assessments or as writing prompts for science journal entries.)

3. Were students able to determine the mathematical relationship between the location of the fulcrum and the distance the weight must be placed from the fulcrum to make the lever balance? (Use observations made during Procedure 4 and on Activity Sheet 8.1 as performance assessments, and use responses to Discussion Question 3 as an embedded assessment.)

4. Did students use the lever concept to build creative science/math mobiles? (Use observations made during Procedure 5 as a performance assessment.)

## RUBRIC 8.1
### Sample rubric using these assessment options

| | Achievement Level | | |
|---|---|---|---|
| | **Developing**<br>**1** | **Proficient**<br>**2** | **Exemplary**<br>**3** |
| Were students able to balance their levers in different ways and explain their techniques? | Attempted to balance their levers but were not particularly successful | Successfully balanced their levers and made a basic explanation of their techniques | Successfully balanced their levers and made a detailed explanation of their techniques, including examples |
| Were students able to explain how the lever and fulcrum interact and how balance is achieved? | Attempted to explain their understanding of the lever, fulcrum, and balance, but were unable to do so to any significant extent | Offered a basic understanding of levers, fulcrum, and balance | Offered a detailed understanding of levers, fulcrum, and balance, and could identify several examples of levers in "real life" |
| Were students able to determine the mathematical relationship between the location of the fulcrum and the distance the weight must be placed from the fulcrum to make the lever balance? | Attempted to determine the relationship but were unable to do so to any significant extent | Successfully recognized the relationship based on their data on Activity Sheet 8.1 | Successfully recognized the relationship based on their data on Activity Sheet 8.1 and could explain it in depth using their numerical data |
| Did students use the lever concept to build creative science/math mobiles? | Attempted, but were unsuccessful | Successfully built a two- or three-layer mobile | Successfully built a four-layer mobile |

# Other Options and Extensions

**1.** Have each student find an adult who uses levers in his or her work. The person could be someone the student knows, or someone he or she learns about on the internet, such as Alexander Calder. What kind of levers does the person use? How are the levers used? How would the person's job be different without levers?

## Resources

Cross, B. 1992. A balancing feat. *Science and Children* 29 (7): 16–17.

Dotger, S. 2008. Using simple machines to leverage learning. *Science and Children* 45 (7): 22–27.

Kirkwood, J. J. 1994. Simple machines simply put. *Science and Children* 31 (7): 15–17, 40–41.

Soares, J., M. L. Blanton, and J. J. Kaput. 2006. Thinking algebraically across the elementary school curriculum. *Teaching Children Mathematics* 12 (5): 228–235.

Streitberger, H. E. 1978. Levers have we got levers. *Science and Children* 16 (3): 9–12.

Williams, D. 1995. *Teaching mathematics through children's art*. Portsmouth, NH: Heinemann.

## ACTIVITY SHEET 8.1
### Learning About Levers

1. Find and list as many ways as possible to make the lever balance without moving or removing the taped weight.

2. Find and list as many ways as possible to make the lever balance without moving the fulcrum from the 45 cm mark.

3. Collect and analyze data to determine the mathematical relationship between the location of the fulcrum and distance the weight must be placed from the fulcrum to make the lever balance.

| Location of Fulcrum | Distance From Weight to Fulcrum |
|---|---|
| 45 cm | _____ cm |
| 40 cm | _____ cm |
| 35 cm | _____ cm |
| 30 cm | _____ cm |
| 25 cm | _____ cm |
| 20 cm | _____ cm |

To balance the lever as the fulcrum is moved farther from the center, the weight must

_____

_____

_____

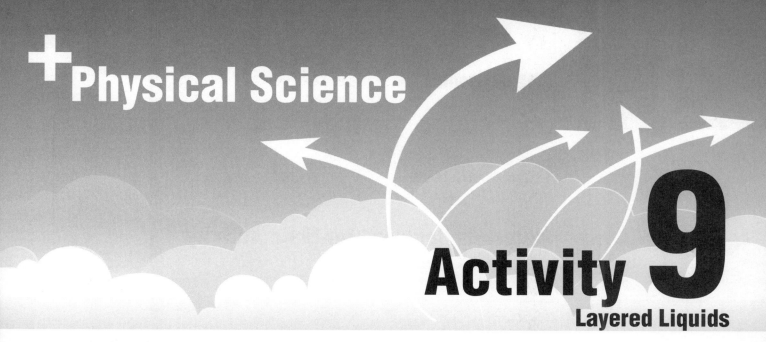

# Physical Science

## Activity 9
### Layered Liquids

## Overview

This activity involves an exploration of density. Why does oil float on water? How does drain cleaner sink down into the clogged pipe right through standing water? These questions will be answered as students make a layered "parfait" of colored liquids based on the varying densities of those liquids. They will calculate densities of the liquid samples as they investigate, describe, and explain the "layered liquids" phenomenon.

## Processes/Skills

- Observing
- Problem solving
- Predicting
- Describing
- Analyzing
- Concluding
- Measuring
- Calculating
- Inquiring
- Communicating
- Cooperating

## Recommended For

*Grades 5–8: Small-group instruction*
To adapt the lesson for fifth graders, you can measure out the 100 ml samples ahead of time and assist with data collection and analysis, or even undertake the investigation as a whole-class activity.

## Time Required

1–2 hours

## Materials Required for Main Activity

- Water
- Food coloring (one color)
- Corn syrup
- Tall, clear, plastic containers (empty water bottles, approximately 500 ml capacity, are just right)
- Beakers or graduated cylinders for measuring liquids
- Paper cups
- Balances
- Calculators
- Maple syrup
- Vegetable oil
- Dishwashing detergent
- Mineral oil

## Connecting to the Standards

### NSES
**Grade 5–8 Content Standards:**

Standard A: Science as Inquiry

- Abilities necessary to do scientific inquiry (especially observing carefully, thinking critically about evidence to develop and communicate good explanations, and using mathematics effectively)
- Understanding about scientific inquiry (especially recognizing the importance of mathematics in science and noticing that scientific explanations emphasize evidence and logically consistent arguments)

Standard B: Physical Science

- Properties and changes of properties in matter (especially investigating density as a property of matter)

**NCTM**
**Standards for Grades 3–8:**

- Numbers and Operations (especially working with numbers and operations to solve problems)

- Measurement (especially understanding and applying the metric system)

- Reasoning and Proof (especially engaging in thinking and reasoning)

- Communication (especially communicating their mathematical thinking clearly)

## Safety Considerations

Basic classroom safety practices apply. Be sure to demonstrate proper handling of the various liquids.

## Activity Objectives

In this activity, students

- layer the four liquid samples and explain their results; and

- determine the layered position of a fifth, unknown, liquid based on its density, which they will calculate.

## Background Information

*Density* is the relative weight of an object, defined mathematically as the object's mass divided by volume. A more dense object or material has more tightly packed internal particles. A brick, for instance, is more dense (that is, has more tightly packed particles within it) than a piece of wood (whose particles are more loosely packed). A brick is more dense than water, and it will sink. Most wood, however, is less dense than water, allowing it to float. Therefore, it is not an object's weight alone that determines whether it will sink or float; it is the object's weight (really its mass) divided by its volume. Consider a large piece of Styrofoam (say, 500 kg): It will float in water despite its large size because it is less dense than the water. That is, it has less mass per unit of volume than water. Or, put another way, if we have two equal volumes (say, 250 cm$^3$) of Styrofoam and of water, the Styrofoam will be lighter in weight (or contain less mass).

## STANDARDS

**SCIENCE**
Abilities necessary to do
  scientific inquiry
Properties and changes of
  properties in matter

**MATH**
Measurement

**MATH**
Numbers and operations

**MATH**
Communication

**SCIENCE**
Understanding about
  scientific inquiry

**MATH**
Reasoning and proof

# Main Activity, Step-by-Step Procedures

1.  Begin this preliminary demonstration by showing the class a two-layered liquid "parfait": water "floating" on corn syrup. (The effect is more dramatic if you first mix a little food coloring into the water and if you let students see you pour the two liquids carefully together.) Ask, "Why do you suppose these liquids form into two layers?" Accept divergent answers, but help students see that density is the reason.

2.  Working together in small, cooperative groups, students begin by measuring out 100 ml each of four different liquids: water, maple syrup, vegetable oil, and dishwashing detergent. Samples must be poured into identical containers (because their masses will be compared); paper cups work well. Students should list the substances by sample number in Activity Sheet 9.1, Table 1, p. 96.

3.  Next, students predict the order of the layers that the four samples will form when poured carefully into the same jar. Which will be on top, and so on? They should record their predictions in Activity Sheet 9.1, Table 2, p. 96.

4.  Using a balance, students measure the mass of each of the samples. (This is why they need to be in identical containers; subtract the mass of the cup, weighed when empty, from the mass of each cup when filled with the liquid sample.) Students should record all data in Activity Sheet 9.1, Table 3, p. 96.

5.  Students should calculate the density of each liquid (mass divided by volume: 100 ml each). Then they should record the densities and again predict the order of the layers that will form when the four samples are poured into the same container (using Activity Sheet 9.1, Table 4, p. 97). Ask students, "Did your prediction change? Why or why not?"

6.  Students should carefully pour the liquids into a single, tall, clear container, one at a time over a spoon so that they don't mix (see Figure 9.1). Then they record the results of the layering effect in Activity Sheet 9.1, Table 5, p. 97. Ask students to explain their results, particularly in relation to their predictions.

7.  Before having students pour out their samples, try this method of performance assessment and/or application of the concepts. Each group receives a fifth liquid sample (for instance, mineral oil; again 100 ml in an identical paper cup). Students must determine where in the layered column the liquid will come to rest by measuring its

mass, calculating its density, and using the density to predict correctly (in Activity Sheet 9.1, Table 6, p. 97). Then students can pour the fifth liquid into the column to check their calculation, analysis, and prediction. They can write science journal entries about how density affects floating and sinking.

## Discussion Questions

Ask students the following:

1. What does density have to do with sinking and floating?

2. If you tried the layering activity aboard the space shuttle in outer space, would the results differ, and if so, how? (The liquids are weightless, so no layers form.) What if you tried the activity on the surface of the Moon? (The liquids would have the same layers as on Earth, despite lower gravitational pull.)

3. Can you think of any jobs that might involve the concepts of density, sinking, and/or floating? Explain your answer for each job that you can name.

**FIGURE 9.1 Pour gently over a spoon to prevent mixing.**

# Assessment

Suggestions for specific ways to assess student understanding are provided in parentheses.

1. Were students able to successfully layer the liquid samples? (Use observations made during Procedures 2–6 as performance assessments.)

2. Were student predictions correct? If so, could students explain why? If not, could they explain why not? (Use Activity Sheet 9.1 as a performance assessment, and use responses to Discussion Questions 1–3 as embedded evidence or as writing prompts for science journal entries.)

3. Could students successfully determine the layered position of the fifth liquid, and did they explain how they arrived at their answer? (Use observations made during Procedure 7 as a performance assessment, and use student analysis of that procedure as a prompt for a science journal entry.)

## RUBRIC 9.1
### Sample rubric using these assessment options

| | Achievement Level | | |
| --- | --- | --- | --- |
| | **Developing**<br>1 | **Proficient**<br>2 | **Exemplary**<br>3 |
| Were students able to successfully layer the liquid samples? | Attempted to layer but were unsuccessful | Successfully measured and layered their liquid samples | Successfully measured and layered their liquid samples and took a leadership role in data collection and analysis |
| Were student predictions correct? If so, could students explain why? If not, could they explain why not? | Attempted to explain their predictions and results but were not able to do so to any significant extent | Effectively explained their predictions, whether accurate or not, in terms of their data and results | Effectively explained their predictions, whether accurate or not, in terms of their data and results, and used math concepts as part of their explanation |
| Could students successfully determine the layered position of the fifth liquid, and did they explain how they arrived at their answers? | Attempted to predict the position of the unknown liquid but were not successful | Successfully predicted the position of the unknown liquid | Successfully predicted the position of the unknown liquid and were able to explain their rationales using math concepts and data examples |

## Other Options and Extensions

**1.** Groups can place some small objects (pieces of wood, cork, rock, eraser, wax, fruit, plastic, metal, etc.) into the layered column (from Procedure 6), predicting where each will come to rest. Students will see that density applies to solid as well as liquid matter.

**2.** Try the basic activity using water and any sort of fruit juice, soda, or other water-based mixture. The distinct layers will not form quickly, if at all (you may need to let the final product settle for several hours before any layering is evident). Ask students to explain why the results differ so significantly from the basic activity. (The fruit juice or soda is composed almost solely of water, so it is neither more nor less dense than the pure water sample. The two samples will mix, and clear layering based on density is not evident.)

## Resources

Beckstead, L. 2008. Science journals: A creative assessment tool. *Science and Children* 46 (3): 22–26.

Bricker, P. 2007. Reinvigorating science journals. *Science and Children* 45 (3): 24–29.

Halpin, M. J., and J. C. Swab. 1990. It's the real thing—The scientific method. *Science and Children* 27 (7): 30–31.

Nesin, G., and L. Barrow. 1984. Density in liquids. *Science and Children* 21 (7): 28–30.

Pearlman, S., and K. Pericak-Spector. 1994. A series of seriation activities. *Science and Children* 31 (4): 37–39.

Scheckel, L. 1993. How to make density float. *Science and Children* 31 (3): 30–33.

## LAYERED LIQUIDS

### ACTIVITY SHEET 9.1
### Layered Liquids

**Table 1**

| Sample | Which Substance? |
|---|---|
| 1 | |
| 2 | |
| 3 | |
| 4 | |

Prediction 1: In what order will the sample layers end up?

**Table 2**

| Layer Order | Sample | Substance |
|---|---|---|
| Top Layer | | |
| Second Layer | | |
| Third Layer | | |
| Bottom Layer | | |

**Table 3**

| Sample | Substance | Mass (Grams) | Volume | Mass/Volume | Density |
|---|---|---|---|---|---|
| 1 | | | 100 ml | /100 ml | |
| 2 | | | 100 ml | /100 ml | |
| 3 | | | 100 ml | /100 ml | |
| 4 | | | 100 ml | /100 ml | |

Prediction 2: After calculating the densities of the samples, what order do you think the final layers will take?

**Table 4**

| Layer Order | Sample | Substance |
|---|---|---|
| Top Layer | | |
| Second Layer | | |
| Third Layer | | |
| Bottom Layer | | |

Results:

**Table 5**

| Layer Order | Sample | Substance |
|---|---|---|
| Top Layer | | |
| Second Layer | | |
| Third Layer | | |
| Bottom Layer | | |

Explain your results:

Data for Sample 5:

**Table 6**

| Sample | Substance | Mass (Grams) | Volume | Mass/Volume | Density |
|---|---|---|---|---|---|
| 5 | | | 100 ml | /100 ml | |

Prediction: Where will the Sample 5 layer be in relation to the other four samples, and how do you know?

Results, using Sample 5:

# Activity 10

## Calculating the Speed of Sound

## Overview

Who hasn't seen a dramatic flash of lightning, only to hear the dramatic "crack" of thunder several seconds later? But why does the thunder reach our ears after we see the lightning? Or, why does the sound of a high-flying jet airplane passing overhead seem to originate far behind the plane itself? The sound and the sight of a distant, loud event are said to be out of phase, that is, they aren't experienced simultaneously. Again, why? In this activity, students will collect data and determine the reason for this phenomenon by calculating the speed of sound and comparing it to the speed of light. In the activity, which can be undertaken with simple materials on any playground or large outdoor area, students will measure, convert units, compare, and reach empirical conclusions based on their own investigation of the phenomenon.

## Processes/Skills

- Observing
- Describing
- Analyzing
- Concluding
- Measuring
- Calculating
- Inquiring
- Communicating
- Cooperating

**CALCULATING THE SPEED OF SOUND**

## Recommended For

*Grades 6–8: Small-group or whole-class instruction*
You can adapt the activity for grades 5 and 6 by undertaking the investigation as a whole-class activity and performing the calculations together.

## Time Required

2–3 hours

## Materials Required for Main Activity

- Calculators
- A hammer and another piece of heavy metal that will make a loud noise when struck with the hammer (A small shovel works well.)
- A clock with sweep second hand
- Metersticks
- Flashlight

## Connecting to the Standards

### NSES
#### Grade 5–8 Content Standards:
Standard A: Science as Inquiry

- Abilities necessary to do scientific inquiry (especially observing carefully, thinking critically about evidence to develop and communicate good explanations, and using mathematics effectively)
- Understanding about scientific inquiry (especially recognizing the importance of mathematics in science and noticing that scientific explanations emphasize evidence and logically consistent arguments)

Standard B: Physical Science

- Transfer of energy (especially investigating the transfer of sound and light energy)

### NCTM
#### Standards for Grades 3–8:

- Numbers and Operations (especially using numbers and operations to solve problems, and developing an understanding of large numbers)

- Algebra (especially using algebra to solve problems)

- Measurement (especially understanding and applying the metric system)

- Reasoning and Proof (especially engaging in thinking and reasoning)

- Communication (especially communicating their mathematical thinking clearly)

- Connections (especially applying mathematics to a scientific investigation)

## Safety Considerations

Basic classroom safety practices apply.

## Activity Objectives

In this activity, students

- collect data regarding the speed of sound;

- calculate and compare their figures for the speed of sound; and

- compare the speed of sound to the speed of light and explain why distant events like thunder and lightning appear to be out of phase.

## Main Activity, Step-by-Step Procedures

1.  Ask students what they know about the speed of sound. Discuss the out-of-phase experiences that the students might have had when they *saw* lightning before they *heard* the thunder or they *saw* a baseball being hit from far away before they actually *heard* the crack of the bat. What other out-of-phase experiences have they had? Expand on these experiences to get at the notion that sound travels at a particular speed, and its speed is less than that of light. Ask students, "How could we measure the speed of sound?"

2.  In this activity, students should work in cooperative groups, but each student should keep his or her own data. First, students must determine the length of their average steps in meters. Place three metersticks on the floor, and each student should measure the length of three steps, recording data on Activity Sheet 10.1, Table 1, p. 107. When students divide the distance by three (the number of steps), they'll arrive at a calculation of meters per step. They should make this measurement and calculation three times, and then divide by three to get an average figure for meters per step. (Run three trials of three steps here because our steps can vary a great deal.)

**SCIENCE**
Abilities necessary to do scientific inquiry

**MATH**
Numbers and operations
Measurement

**MATH**
Algebra

**3.** The next step in the procedure will take you and the class outside to any large, open area on the school grounds. Before going out, be sure that students know what is expected of them during this "field trip." Once outside, begin hitting any handy piece of metal (such as the blade of a short-handled shovel) with a hammer, making a loud "bang." You must make contact with the hammer once every second, using the sweep second hand of a wristwatch on your stationary arm to time your strikes. The trick here is to move your arm crisply and mechanically in an arclike motion, so that the hammer is clearly at one end of the arc every half second. At one half second, the hammer is clearly away from the shovel, and at the next half second it is contacting the shovel with a bang (see Figure 10.1).

Once you find your rhythm, have the students walk away, moving backward. When they are close, the sound and the sight of the hammer blow will be simultaneous, but as they move farther away from you the sound and sight will become increasingly out of phase. They must keep moving away until the sound and sight of the blow are one-half second out of phase, that is, until they hear the bang when the hammer is at the opposite end of the arc (i.e., hammer position B in Figure 10.1). Then students walk back to your position, counting the number of steps that they take to return to you (because you are the source of the sound). The number of steps should be recorded on Activity Sheet 10.1, Table 2, p. 107, and the procedure should be repeated three times.

**FIGURE 10.1. Make contact and loud noise, at 1-second intervals (position A). Then move your arm crisply to position B at the 0.5-second mark.**

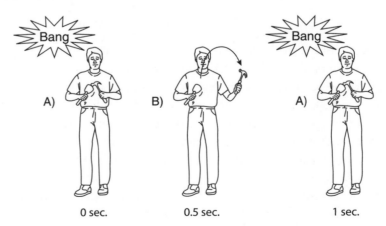

A)            B)            A)

0 sec.        0.5 sec.        1 sec.

**STANDARDS**

**SCIENCE**
Understanding about
  scientific inquiry
Transfer of energy

**MATH**
Reasoning and proof
Communication
Connections

4. When you have returned to the classroom, the students can begin their calculations for the speed of sound using Activity Sheet 10.1, Table 3, p. 107. The first task is to determine the distance, in meters, that they stepped off in Procedure 2. They need to multiply the number of steps (for each of the three trials from Procedure 2) times the average number of meters per step determined in Procedure 1. This will give the speed that sound travels in one-half second (because the distance measured was based on the hammer's sound and sight being one-half second out of phase). To get the speed of sound per second, simply multiply by two.

   To summarize the calculation: distance in steps (from Procedure 2) times number of meters per step (from Procedure 1) times two = the speed of sound in meters per second.

   Or put another way: distance (steps/0.5 sec) × m/step × 2 (0.5 sec/sec) = speed of sound (m/sec)

5. After calculating the speed based on each of the three trials, find an average of the three for a final figure. Students can easily convert the speed of sound from meters per second into feet per second using Activity Sheet 10.1, Table 4, p. 108. Because there are 39.37 in./m, and 12 in./ft., just multiply the speed of sound (that is, from Procedure 3 the average of the three trials, in meters per second) times 39.37 in./m, divided by 12 in./ft. The result will be the speed of sound in feet per second.

   To summarize the calculation: speed of sound (m/sec) × 39.37 in./m ÷ 12 in./ft. = speed of sound (ft./sec)

6. At this point, students can compare their results and discuss what they've learned about sound. Explore the following questions with the class: How did the students' values for the speed of sound compare with the "official" value (343 m/sec or 1,125 ft./sec)? (Any student values that come within a factor of 10 are quite impressive, given the margin for error in this investigation.) What was the class average? How do students account for the differences between their values and the "official" value? What were the sources of error in their procedures? How could they obtain a more accurate figure for the speed of sound? What problems did they have with the calculations? What did they learn about sound? What else would they like to know?

7. So, why do we see the lightning before we hear the thunder? Shine a flashlight around the classroom, clicking it off and on repeatedly.

Consider comparing the speed of sound to the speed of light (i.e., Why do we see something in the distance, such as lightning, before we hear it?). Light travels at 299,324 km/sec. or 186,000 mi./sec. To convert these figures into the appropriate units for comparison with the calculated speed of sound (meters per second), multiply 299,324 km/sec. times 1,000 m/km to get the speed in meters per second. Multiply 186,000 mi./sec. times 5,280 ft./mi. to get feet per second. Record all figures in the appropriate spaces on Activity Sheet 10.1. Once students compare the speed of sound with the speed of light, they should be able to explain why we see distant events (like lightning) before we hear them. (Because the light from an event travels much faster than the sound.)

## Discussion Questions

Ask students the following:

1.  How accurate was your calculation of the speed of sound? Can you think of any sources of error that led to inaccuracies? If you were going to determine the speed of sound again, what, if anything, would you do differently?

2.  Why is it that you see a distant event, like lightning, before you hear it?

3.  What else would you like to know about sound and how it travels?

## Assessment

Suggestions for specific ways to assess student understanding are provided in parentheses.

1.  Were students able to successfully collect step data during their "field trip"? (Use observations made during Procedures 2 and 3 and Activity Sheet 10.1 as performance assessments.)

2.  Could students calculate and compare their figures for the speed of sound? (Use Activity Sheet 10.1 as a performance assessment.)

3.  Were students able to compare the speed of sound to the speed of light and explain why distant events like thunder and lightning appear to be out of phase? (Use student responses to Discussion Questions 1–3 as embedded assessments or as writing prompts for science journal entries.)

**RUBRIC 10.1**
**Sample rubric using these assessment options**

| | Achievement Level | | |
| --- | --- | --- | --- |
| | Developing<br>1 | Proficient<br>2 | Exemplary<br>3 |
| Were students able to successfully collect step data during their "field trip"? | Attempted to collect step data but were not successful | Successfully collected step data for use in calculations | Successfully collected step data and were able to explain rationales for the process |
| Could students calculate and compare their figures for the speed of sound? | Attempted to calculate and compare their figures but were not successful | Successfully calculated and compared their figures | Successfully calculated and compared their figures and were able to explain the mathematical operations used |
| Were students able to compare the speed of sound to the speed of light and explain why distant events like thunder and lightning appear to be out of phase? | Attempted to explain but were unsuccessful to any significant extent | Successfully explained the out-of-phase phenomenon | Successfully explained the out-of-phase phenomenon and did so using mathematical details |

# Other Options and Extensions

1. Have students research the history of the speed of sound and how scientists originally calculated it. How did their methods compare with yours in this activity?

2. Have students determine whether people can travel at or beyond the speed of sound.

3. Have students find out what causes a sonic boom.

4. Have students find out how the speed of light was determined. How did their methods compare with your method of calculating the speed of sound in this actitivity?

5. Have students determine whether people can travel at or beyond the speed of light.

## Resources

Beckstead, L. 2008. Science journals: A creative assessment tool. *Science and Children* 46 (3): 22–26.

Klamik, A. 2006. Converting customary units. *Teaching Children Mathematics* 13 (3): 188–191.

Macrorie, K. 1984. *20 teachers*. New York: Oxford University Press.

Schaffer, L., H. Pinson, and T. Kokoski. 1998. Listening to rain sticks. *Science and Children* 35 (5): 22–27.

Soares, J., M. L. Blanton, and J. J. Kaput. 2006. Thinking algebraically across the elementary school curriculum. *Teaching Children Mathematics* 12 (5): 228–235.

## ACTIVITY SHEET 10.1
### Calculating the Speed of Sound

**1.** Calculate the average number of meters per step.

**Table 1**

| Trials | Distance (in Meters) | | Meters per Step |
|---|---|---|---|
| 1 - Three Steps | | ÷ 3 | |
| 2 - Three Steps | | ÷ 3 | |
| 3 - Three Steps | | ÷ 3 | |
| | | | Average: |

**2.** Record the distance from 0.5 seconds out of phase to the sound source (from "field trip").

**Table 2**

| Trial | Distance (in Steps) |
|---|---|
| 1 | _____ Steps |
| 2 | _____ Steps |
| 3 | _____ Steps |

**3.** Calculate the speed of sound in meters per second.

**Table 3**

| Distances in Steps (From Table 2) | Average Meters per Step (From Table 1) | | Speed of Sound in Meters per Second |
|---|---|---|---|
| _____ Steps | × _____ m/step | × 2 | |
| _____ Steps | × _____ m/step | × 2 | |
| _____ Steps | × _____ m/step | × 2 | |
| | | | Average: |

4. Convert the speed of sound from meters per second to feet per second.

**Table 4**

| Speed of Sound in Meters per Second (From Table 3) | 39.37 Inches per Meter | 12 Inches per Foot | Speed of Sound in Feet per Second |
|---|---|---|---|
| | × 39.37 | ÷ 12 | |
| | × 39.37 | ÷ 12 | |
| | × 39.37 | ÷ 12 | |
| | | | Average: |

5. What have you learned about the speed of sound?

6. Compare the speed of sound to the speed of light.

| Speed of Light (in Km per Second) | | Speed of Light (in Meters per Second) |
|---|---|---|
| 299,324 | × 1,000 m/km | |

| Speed of Light (in Miles per Second) | | Speed of Light (in Feet per Second) |
|---|---|---|
| 186,000 | × 5,280 ft. /mi. | |

| Speed of Light (in Meters per Second) | |
|---|---|
| Speed of Sound (in Meters per Second) | |

| Speed of Light (in Feet per Second) | |
|---|---|
| Speed of Sound (in Feet per Second) | |

Why is it that you sometimes see a distant event before you hear the noise it makes (like seeing lightning before you hear the thunder)?

# +Chemical Science

# Activity 11

## Exploring the Dynamics of Temperature

## Overview

Would your students like to take care of a penguin? To be a penguin-sitter, they would have to know what conditions that bird needs to survive. One important factor would be temperature. In this activity, you will challenge student groups to prove that they could care for a penguin by demonstrating they can maintain the temperature of a glass of water at 10°C (using ice and/or body heat from their hands) for 15 minutes, recording the temperature every 30 seconds, and graphing their data. By reflecting on the procedure, students will learn about the dynamics of a closed system, the nature of water, and the value of adjusting to fluctuating environmental conditions.

## Processes/Skills

- Reading a thermometer
- Graphing
- Analyzing data
- Observing
- Predicting
- Measuring
- Describing
- Inferring
- Experimenting
- Communicating
- Comparing
- Reflecting

- Inquiring
- Recognizing patterns
- Problem solving
- Cooperating

## Recommended For

*Grades 5–8: Small-group or whole-class instruction*
Encourage fifth graders by suggesting methods, during Procedure 3, for adjusting the water temperature, such as inserting their warm fingers carefully into the water.

## Time Required

1–2 hours

## Materials Required for Main Activity

- Three plastic or paper cups that will hold at least 250 ml of liquid
- Ice (cubes or chips—enough for each group to have a cupful)
- Water
- Large (at least 250 ml) plastic drinking cups
- Several 500 ml beakers
- Graph paper
- Alcohol-filled thermometers or temperature probes for computer or graphing calculator

## Connecting to the Standards

### NSES
**Grade 5–8 Content Standards:**
Standard A: Science as Inquiry

- Abilities necessary to do scientific inquiry (especially observing carefully, thinking critically about evidence to develop and communicate good explanations, and using mathematics effectively)

- Understanding about scientific inquiry (especially recognizing the importance of mathematics in science and noticing that scientific explanations emphasize evidence and logically consistent arguments)

Standard B: Physical Science

- Transfer of energy (especially that heat flows from warmer objects to cooler ones)

Standard C: Life Science

- Structure and function in living systems (especially that structure and function are complementary)

- Regulation and behavior (especially that organisms maintain stable internal conditions within a changing external environment)

- Diversity and adaptations of organisms (especially regarding biological adaptations that enhance species survival)

### NCTM
**Standards for Grades 3–8:**

- Measurement (especially understanding and applying the metric system)

- Data Analysis and Probability (especially displaying relevant data to answer questions)

- Reasoning and Proof (especially engaging in thinking and reasoning)

- Communication (especially communicating their mathematical thinking clearly)

## Safety Considerations

Basic classroom safety practices apply. If you use alcohol-filled thermometers (don't use mercury-filled thermometers), be sure to choose those with metal safety backs.

## Activity Objectives

In this activity, students

- maintain a cup of water in a state of dynamic thermal equilibrium and explain how they did so;

- graph, explain, and compare their data; and

- identify examples of dynamic equilibria in everyday life.

**STANDARDS**

**MATH**
Measurement

## Main Activity, Step-by-Step Procedures

1. Show the class three cups: one containing water at room temperature, one containing warm water, and one containing ice water. Ask student volunteers to touch each cup and describe how it feels. Then have student volunteers measure the temperature of the water in each cup using thermometers. Be sure that all students understand how to read and use the thermometer. Ask the class where in the world we might find warm water, cold water, and room-temperature water. It will be helpful here to refer to a map or globe. On the chalkboard, make a chart with columns headed "Warm Water," "Cold Water," and "Room-Temperature Water." As a class, brainstorm locations on the map that students think would fall under one of the headings and list them on the chart. Also brainstorm and list the sorts of animals that students think might live in each of those three water temperature categories.

2. Ask students to use their imaginations as you describe the following scenario: *A friend recently returned from Antarctica and brought with her a young penguin for the local zoo. She has asked you to penguin-sit for 15 minutes, but she wants to be sure that you can keep the penguin comfortable. This particular bird likes to be kept at a constant temperature of 10°C. Working with your group, you will start with a cup of water at room temperature. Your challenge is to alter the water temperature to 10°C as quickly as possible using ice, and then to keep it there for the remainder of the 15 minutes. You must record your progress at 30-second intervals, graph your results, and present your observations and conclusions to the class.*

3. Working in groups of four, students prepare for the activity. To ensure that duties are shared, members assume specific tasks: materials specialist, thermometer specialist, data specialist, and graph specialist. Using a 500 ml beaker, the materials specialist must measure out 200 ml of tap water into the cup. The thermometer specialist places the thermometer into the water and waits several minutes until it has adjusted to the initial water temperature and registers that temperature. The data specialist records that initial temperature on Activity Sheet 11.1, p. 119, and keeps track of timing for the duration of the 15-minute activity. (If you have a limited number of watches, you may prefer to be the timekeeper for the entire class, calling out the 30-second intervals for all.) The graph specialist is responsible for troubleshooting during the activity and for creating a graph of the temperature data once the observations are completed (plotting time on the *x* axis and temperature on the *y* axis).

**STANDARDS**

**SCIENCE**
Abilities necessary to do
 scientific inquiry
Transfer of energy

**MATH**
Data analysis and
 probability

**SCIENCE**
Understanding about
 scientific inquiry
Structure and function in
 living systems
Regulation and behavior
Diversity and adaptations
 of organisms

**MATH**
Reasoning and proof
Communication

**4.** Before beginning the activity itself, discuss how to raise and lower the water temperature. Students may suggest methods such as adding and/or removing ice, wrapping their hands around the cup, or inserting their fingers into the water. *They may not, however, remove any liquid water from the cup.* Allow them several minutes to determine their thermal strategies. Ask students to predict what will happen during the activity and to write their predictions at the top of Activity Sheet 11.1.

**5.** Once the initial room temperature thermometer reading has been made and recorded, the materials specialist adds ice to the cup of water to drop the temperature as quickly as possible. Every 30 seconds for the next 15 minutes the data specialist records the temperature reported by the thermometer specialist. When the temperature drops below 10°C, the cup must have ice removed and/or be warmed. When it rises above 10°C, the cup must be cooled with more ice. When all the data are recorded, the graph specialist makes the graph of time versus temperature and the group members make conclusions about their findings. Students should address how their predictions differed from their results.

**6.** As a class, compare the groups' graphs, looking for similarities, differences, and patterns. Usually, graphs will indicate a radical decrease to below 10°C, followed by an increase to above 10°C, and then have minor fluctuation around the 10° mark for the remainder of the 15 minutes. Also, discuss the methods used by the various groups to try to maintain the temperature. Students are commonly surprised to find that, at least initially, it is difficult to maintain a stable 10°C temperature. They realize that they need to make ongoing thermal adjustments to keep the water temperature relatively stable. Introduce the concept of *dynamic equilibrium*, explaining that the term refers to the way a system, such as their cup of water, is constantly affected by cooling and warming influences, yet seems to remain at a fairly constant temperature. We use the word *dynamic* because the temperature is always changing and *equilibrium* because nonetheless it tends to remain in balance. The apparent lack of overall temperature change is caused by a balance of the heating and cooling influences, creating a state of dynamic equilibrium. Dynamic equilibria are found in many situations (not all of which involve heat), including trying to drive a car in a straight line, thermal regulation of the human body, the human appetite, the temperature of a room when it is maintained by a thermostat, and the complementary processes of evaporation and condensation of water in a closed container (such as a terrarium).

Ask students how they think penguins maintain a stable body temperature (that is, their dynamic thermal equilibrium) in extremely cold environmental conditions. Explain that penguins have three main strategies: (1) *anatomical adaptations* such as feathers for insulation, their general shape (which minimizes heat loss), and their layer of insulating body fat; (2) *behavioral adaptations* such as huddling together in colonies; and (3) *metabolic adaptations* such as maintaining a very high body temperature. Ask students, "How do you adapt to very cold weather? How do you adapt to very warm weather?"

## Discussion Questions

Ask students the following:

1. How can penguins adapt to constant changes in environmental temperature? How do they adjust to colder or warmer water?

2. What sorts of problems did you run into when trying to maintain the water temperature?

3. Can you think of other examples of dynamic equilibria in the real world? That is, can you think of any other systems that seem to be constant but are actually constantly fluctuating?

4. How effectively did you work as a group? Did any problems arise among group members? How did you solve those problems?

## Assessment

Suggestions for specific ways to assess student understanding are provided in parentheses.

1. Were the students able to maintain the cup of water in a state of dynamic thermal equilibrium? Were they able to describe the technique(s) used to do so? (Use your observations during Procedure 5 and Activity Sheet 11.1 as performance assessments, and use Discussion Questions 1 and 2 as embedded assessments.)

2. Were students able to graph and explain their data? (Use Procedures 5 and 6 and Activity Sheet 11.1 as performance assessments.)

3. Were students able to identify similarities and differences among the class's graphs? Could they explain what was represented by the graphs? (Use Procedure 6 and Activity Sheet 11.1 as performance assessments.)

4. Could students identify other examples of dynamic equilibria? (Use responses to Discussion Question 3 as embedded assessments.)

**RUBRIC 11.1**
**Sample rubric using these assessment options**

| | Achievement Level | | |
|---|---|---|---|
| | **Developing 1** | **Proficient 2** | **Exemplary 3** |
| Were the students able to maintain the cup of water in a state of dynamic thermal equilibrium? Were they able to describe the technique(s) used to do so? | Attempted to maintain a dynamic thermal equilibrium but were not successful | Successfully maintained a dynamic thermal equilibrium and were able to offer a basic description of their techniques | Successfully maintained a dynamic thermal equilibrium and were able to offer detailed descriptions of their techniques, including explanations of why their techniques worked |
| Were students able to graph and explain their data? | Attempted to graph and explain their data but were not successful | Successfully graphed and explained their data | Successfully graphed and explained their data in detail, including appropriate terminology |
| Were students able to identify similarities and differences among the class's graphs? Could they explain what was represented by the graphs? | Attempted to compare graphs but were not successful | Successfully compared graphs and offered a basic explanation of what the graph represented | Successfully compared graphs and offered detailed explanations of what the graphs represented, including appropriate terminology |
| Could students identify other examples of dynamic equilibria? | Attempted to identify other examples of dynamic equilibria but were not successful | Successfully identified several examples of dynamic equilibria | Successfully identified several examples of dynamic equilibria and explained them in detail using appropriate terminology |

# Other Options and Extensions

1. Have students find out more about how penguins and other aquatic animals or plants adapt to their thermal environments.

2. Explore this question with the class: How does the role played by your blood (a fluid) in regulating your body's thermal equilibrium resemble the role played by the oceans (another fluid) in regulating global climates?

3. Have students research polar exploration, human living conditions in polar regions, and ethical questions regarding the use of arctic and antarctic resources.

**4.** Have students find out more about the physiology of warm-blooded and cold-blooded animals.

## Resources

Biological Sciences Curriculum Study. 1994. *Middle school science and technology: Investigating systems and change*. Dubuque, IA: Kendall/Hunt.

Buczynski, S. 2006. What's hot? What's not? *Science and Children* 44 (2): 25–29.

Chick, L., A. S. Holmes, N. McClymonds, S. Musick, P. Reynolds, and P. Shultz. 2008. Weather or not. *Teaching Children Mathematics* 14 (8): 464–465.

Eichinger, J. 1996. Science is constantly cool. *Science and Children* 33 (7): 25–27, 43.

Heating up, cooling down. 2005. *Science and Children* 42 (8): 47–48.

Lucas, S. B. 1976. Crystals, snowflakes, and frost. *Science and Children* 14 (2): 16–17.

Moore, D. A. 1999. Some like it hot. *Teaching Children Mathematics* 5: 538–543.

Roth, W. 1989. Experimenting with temperature probes. *Science and Children* 27 (3): 52–54.

Royce, C. A. 2005. Antarctic adaptations. *Science and Children* 42 (4): 16–18.

Urban-Rich, J. 2006. The polar insulation investigation. *Science and Children* 44 (2): 20–24.

## ACTIVITY SHEET 11.1
### Exploring the Dynamics of Temperature

**1.** Prediction: What do you think will happen to the water temperature over the 15-minute period?

_____

_____

**2.** Record your data in the table below.
(Starting time: _____:_____)

| | Time | Temperature (°C) |
|---|---|---|
| 1 | 0 min. 0 sec. | |
| 2 | 0 min. 30 sec. | |
| 3 | 1 min. 0 sec. | |
| 4 | 1 min. 30 sec. | |
| 5 | 2 min. 0 sec. | |
| 6 | 2 min. 30 sec. | |
| 7 | 3 min. 0 sec. | |
| 8 | 3 min. 30 sec. | |
| 9 | 4 min. 0 sec. | |
| 10 | 4 min. 30 sec. | |
| 11 | 5 min. 0 sec. | |
| 12 | 5 min. 30 sec. | |
| 13 | 6 min. 0 sec. | |
| 14 | 6 min. 30 sec. | |
| 15 | 7 min. 0 sec. | |
| 16 | 7 min. 30 sec. | |
| 17 | 8 min. 0 sec. | |
| 18 | 8 min. 30 sec. | |
| 19 | 9 min. 0 sec. | |
| 20 | 9 min. 30 sec. | |
| 21 | 10 min. 0 sec. | |

| 22 | 10 min. 30 sec. | |
|----|----|----|
| 23 | 11 min. 0 sec. | |
| 24 | 11 min. 30 sec. | |
| 25 | 12 min. 0 sec. | |
| 26 | 12 min. 30 sec. | |
| 27 | 13 min. 0 sec. | |
| 28 | 13 min. 30 sec. | |
| 29 | 14 min. 0 sec. | |
| 30 | 14 min. 30 sec. | |
| 31 | 15 min. 0 sec. | |

**3.** What techniques did your group use to maintain a stable 10°C temperature for the 15-minute period?

**4.** Graph your data (time on the *x* axis and temperature on the *y* axis).

**5.** What can you conclude about keeping a cup of water at a stable temperature, based on your data?

**6.** How did your predictions differ from your actual results? How do you know?

# Chemical Science

## Activity 12
### Observing the Effects of Acids and Bases

## Overview
Combining acid/base chemistry, cell biology, and quantitative research methods, this "egg-ceptional" activity promotes a truly interdisciplinary perspective. First, students find out what effect acids and bases have on calcium-based substances such as eggshell and bone. Second, they discover what changes occur when decalcified eggs are placed in solutions of water and corn syrup. Throughout the two exercises, student groups will be measuring, analyzing, and using data to reach valid conclusions.

## Processes/Skills
- Observing
- Predicting
- Measuring
- Calculating
- Graphing
- Analyzing
- Questioning
- Comparing
- Describing
- Cooperating
- Communicating
- Making conclusions based on data

## Recommended For

*Grades 6–8: Small-group instruction*
Adaptations for grade 6 might include collecting, graphing, and analyzing the data as a whole class.

## Time Required

2–3 hours

## Materials Required for Main Activity

- Splash-proof safety goggles
- Chicken eggs
- Chicken bones
- Metersticks
- String
- Balances
- Beakers/measuring cups
- Graduated cylinders/measuring spoons
- Vinegar
- Water
- Baking soda
- Large plastic cups (≥ 500 ml capacity)
- Paper towels
- Corn syrup
- Calculators
- Graph paper

## Connecting to the Standards

### NSES
### Grade 5–8 Content Standards:
Standard A: Science as Inquiry

- Abilities necessary to do scientific inquiry (especially observing care-

fully, thinking critically about evidence to develop and communicate good explanations, and using mathematics effectively)

- Understanding about scientific inquiry (especially recognizing the importance of mathematics in science and noticing that scientific explanations emphasize evidence and logically consistent arguments)

Standard B: Physical Science

- Properties and changes of properties in matter (especially regarding the characteristic properties of substances)

Standard C: Life Science

- Structure and function in living systems (especially that structure and function are complementary)

- Diversity and adaptation of organisms (especially regarding biological adaptations that enhance species survival)

### NCTM
### Standards for Grades 3–8:

- Measurement (especially understanding and applying the metric system)

- Data Analysis and Probability (especially displaying relevant data to answer questions)

- Reasoning and Proof (especially engaging in thinking and reasoning)

## Safety Considerations

Basic classroom safety practices apply. Splash-proof safety goggles must be worn at all times during this activity. When working with the vinegar and water solution, chemical-resistant gloves and apron should be worn.

## Activity Objectives

In this activity, students

- describe the changes in eggs and bones caused by acids and bases and explain why those changes took place; and

- discern and explain the differences between decalcified eggs in water and in corn syrup based on their measurements and data analyses.

## SCIENCE
Abilities necessary to do
scientific inquiry
Properties and changes of
properties in matter

## MATH
Measurement

## SCIENCE
Structure and function in
living systems
Diversity and adaptation
of organisms

## SCIENCE
Understanding about
scientific inquiry

## Main Activity, Step-by-Step Procedures

1. Begin by asking students what effect they think a weak acid or a weak base will have on an egg or a chicken bone if the egg or bone is soaked in either solution for three days. Encourage diverse responses and ask for students' rationales. Give each student group two fresh eggs and a chicken bone (leg bones work best here) and direct them to measure the eggs (length and width using a meterstick; circumference using a string and meterstick; mass using a balance) and the bone (length and mass only), recording their data on Activity Sheet 12.1, p. 129. Students should then predict and record what they think will happen to each of the objects in each of the solutions over the next three days.

2. Wearing safety goggles (which should be worn throughout this activity), students can then prepare the two solutions needed, or the teacher can prepare them as the class observes. The first is acid, using vinegar (acetic acid): mixed 50:50, vinegar to water. The second is base, using baking soda: 30 g, which is about 15 ml or one tablespoon, mixed into 250 ml, or a cup, of water. Place both an egg and the chicken bone into the same container of vinegar solution. Place the other egg into the basic solution and wait three days. (Students can look at the progress over the three-day period, but they shouldn't touch the specimens.)

3. After the 72-hour wait, student groups should remove all three objects from the solutions, gently blotting each dry with a paper towel. Using Activity Sheet 12.1 to record data, students should describe and remeasure each object. Ask students, "How have the eggs changed? Which solution (the acid or the base) caused the greatest change? How did the bone change? Can you explain your observations?" Explain to the class that the acid caused *decalcification*, that is, it removed the calcium from the eggshell and from the bone. It is calcium that makes bones, shells, and teeth hard. (Here is a good opportunity to discuss calcium in the diet, the importance of dental hygiene, and so on.) The base does not cause decalcification, as the second egg should demonstrate. The bone, when decalcified, can even be tied in a knot!

4. Explain that the hard, calcified shell protects the fragile egg inside. Just inside the shell, however, is a thin membrane containing the egg. When the shell has been leached away by the acid, this membrane becomes evident. It holds the egg together. It also controls the

**STANDARDS**

**MATH**
Data analysis and
  probability
Reasoning and proof

flow of materials into and out of the egg. The membrane, as well as the shell, have tiny pores that allow materials to pass in and out. A membrane that allows materials to pass through it is known as a *permeable* membrane, and the flow of substances across the membrane is called *osmosis*.

Student groups now will take their decalcified eggs and place them into containers of either water or corn syrup, as directed by the teacher (half the eggs in one liquid and half in the other). Students should be sure that the eggs are gently blotted, weighed, and measured before placing them into the assigned liquids. (Measurements are recorded on Activity Sheet 12.2, p. 130.) The eggs will be soaked for 30 minutes. At 10-minute intervals, students must remove the eggs from the liquid, gently blot them dry, and record their mass, length, width, and circumference. As a means of comparison (i.e., a control), each group should also undertake the same procedure with a normal egg, complete with shell.

5. When all student groups have completed the 30-minute task, groups can compare their data for the decalcified eggs. They should also graph the class averages of the egg mass data (on the *y* axis) versus time (the 10-minute intervals, on the *x* axis). Have students plot the egg-in-water and egg-in-syrup data on the same graph for easier comparison. Ask students, "Were the eggs affected differently by the two liquids? Can you offer explanations for their results?" Explain that *osmosis* occurred in the decalcified eggs; that is, water moved through the membrane either into or out of the egg. The water moves through the membrane from higher to lower concentration. That is, in the syrup, the water moved out of the egg, causing it to lose mass (because there was a higher concentration of water inside the egg, when compared with the outer syrup—the water coming out of the egg attempted to "dilute" the corn syrup to create a balance of molecules on either side of the membrane). The egg in water enlarged, however, because water moved into it (because the inside of the egg had a lower concentration of water when compared with the water bath in which it soaked—again attempting to create a balance by "diluting" the liquid inside the egg). Ask students, "Did you observe any changes in the normal egg? How can the changes be explained?" (The shell protects the egg from osmosis.)

You might add that most living tissues have membranes and undergo osmosis. In fact, when we bathe for a long time our skin cells swell with water (as the water tries to "dilute" us by osmotically passing through our skin cell membranes). When we get out of the bath, we begin to lose the water we gained, and our stretched and previously swollen skin wrinkles. This shriveling is particularly apparent on our hands and fingers.

6. Find out if students have any questions of their own about the effect of acids and bases, decalcification, or osmosis. Offer research ideas so that they might find their answers.

## Discussion Questions

Ask students the following:

1. How do acids and bases affect such materials as eggs and bones? Why does this happen?

2. If you wanted to make a decalcified egg grow larger, what sort of liquid could you put it in? How do you know?

3. Why is osmosis important to a chicken egg? Why is osmosis important to living cells?

4. Why is a shell important to an egg? How do you know?

## Assessment

Suggestions for specific ways to assess student understanding are provided in parentheses.

1. Were students able to effectively describe the changes in eggs and bones and to explain why the changes took place? (Use Activity Sheet 12.1 as a performance assessment, and use student responses to Discussion Questions 1 and 4 as embedded assessments or as writing prompts for science journal entries.)

2. Were students able to discern and explain the differences between decalcified eggs in water and in corn syrup based on their measurements and data analyses? (Use Activity Sheet 12.2 as a performance assessment, and use student responses to Discussion Questions 3 and 4 as embedded assessments or as writing prompts for science journal entries.)

**RUBRIC 12.1**
**Sample rubric using these assessment options**

| | Achievement Level | | |
| --- | --- | --- | --- |
| | Developing 1 | Proficient 2 | Exemplary 3 |
| Were students able to effectively describe the changes in eggs and bones and to explain why the changes took place? | Attempted to describe the changes, but were unable to do so to any significant extent | Successfully described the changes and why they occurred | Successfully described, in detail, with examples and use of appropriate terminology, the changes and why they occurred |
| Were students able to discern and explain the differences between decalcified eggs in water and in corn syrup based on their measurements and data analyses? | Attempted to describe the differences but were unable to do so to any significant extent | Successfully described the differences and why they occurred | Successfully described, in detail, with examples and use of appropriate terminology, the differences and why they occurred |

# Other Options and Extensions

1.  Have students try to decalcify eggs in other weak acids (e.g., orange juice).

2.  Encourage students to try another experiment in which they put water-soluble dyes (e.g., methylene blue, methyl green, or safranine O—all available through biological supply catalogs) into water with decalcified eggs. Students should determine why the eggs will take on the color of the dyes. Then have students explain why food coloring will not pass through the eggs' membranes.

3.  Have students research how an amphibian's eggs differ from bird or reptile eggs and how those differences affect how amphibians live.

## Resources

Chambless, M. S., S. Blackwell, C. Redding, and A. Oswalt. 1998. A data "eggs"ploration. *Teaching Children Mathematics* 4: 448–451.

Cocanour, B., and A. S. Bruce. 1986. The case of the soft-shelled egg. *Science and Children* 23 (6): 13–14.

Cooper, G., and S. M. Lonsdale. 1986. Eggs and science in Katmandu. *Science and Children* 24 (6): 18–19.

Damonte, K. 2004. Understanding acid rain. *Science and Children* 42 (3): 53–54.

MacKinnon, G. R. 1998. Soap and science. *Science and Children* 35 (5): 28–31.

Robertson, B. 2006. Why does a color change indicate a chemical change? *Science and Children* 43 (5): 48–49.

Sullivan, A. 1989. Acid basics. *Science and Children* 27 (2): 22–24.

Townsend, J., and K. Bunton. 2006. Indicators for inquiry. *Science and Children* 43 (5): 37–41.

Yang, D. 2006. Developing number sense through real-life situations in school. *Teaching Children Mathematics* 13 (2): 104–106.

**Activity Sheet 12.1**

## OBSERVING THE EFFECTS OF ACIDS AND BASES

| | Predicted Changes | Measurements Before | Measurements After | Description of Any Changes |
|---|---|---|---|---|
| Eggs in Vinegar (Acid) | | Length: ——— mm<br>Width: ——— mm<br>Circumference: ——— mm<br>Mass: ——— g | Length: ——— mm<br>Width: ——— mm<br>Circumference: ——— mm<br>Mass: ——— g | |
| Eggs in Baking Soda (Base) | | Length: ——— mm<br>Width: ——— mm<br>Circumference: ——— mm<br>Mass: ——— g | Length: ——— mm<br>Width: ——— mm<br>Circumference: ——— mm<br>Mass: ——— g | |
| Bone in Vinegar (Acid) | | Length: ——— mm<br>Width: ——— mm<br>Circumference: ——— mm<br>Mass: ——— g | Length: ——— mm<br>Width: ——— mm<br>Circumference: ——— mm<br>Mass: ——— g | |

How do you explain the changes in the eggs and/or bone?

## ACTIVITY SHEET 12.2
## Observing the Effects of Acids and Bases Over Time

| Predicted Changes | Starting Measurements | After 10 Minutes | After 20 Minutes | After 30 Minutes |
|---|---|---|---|---|
| Decalcified egg in water | Length: ____ mm<br>Width: ____ mm<br>Circumference: ____ mm<br>Mass: ____ g | Length: ____ mm<br>Width: ____ mm<br>Circumference: ____ mm<br>Mass: ____ g | Length: ____ mm<br>Width: ____ mm<br>Circumference: ____ mm<br>Mass: ____ g | Length: ____ mm<br>Width: ____ mm<br>Circumference: ____ mm<br>Mass: ____ g |
| Decalcified egg in corn syrup | Length: ____ mm<br>Width: ____ mm<br>Circumference: ____ mm<br>Mass: ____ g | Length: ____ mm<br>Width: ____ mm<br>Circumference: ____ mm<br>Mass: ____ g | Length: ____ mm<br>Width: ____ mm<br>Circumference: ____ mm<br>Mass: ____ g | Length: ____ mm<br>Width: ____ mm<br>Circumference: ____ mm<br>Mass: ____ g |
| Normal egg with shell | Length: ____ mm<br>Width: ____ mm<br>Circumference: ____ mm<br>Mass: ____ g | Length: ____ mm<br>Width: ____ mm<br>Circumference: ____ mm<br>Mass: ____ g | Length: ____ mm<br>Width: ____ mm<br>Circumference: ____ mm<br>Mass: ____ g | Length: ____ mm<br>Width: ____ mm<br>Circumference: ____ mm<br>Mass: ____ g |

How do you explain the changes in the eggs?

# Activity 13
## Discovering Sand and Sand Paintings

## Overview

This activity blends social studies and art with math and science. First, students will explore the visible characteristics of sand, and then they will make Navajo-style sand paintings with paper, glue, and colored sand. In the process, they will hone their estimation skills by assessing the number of sand grains on their paintings, as well as in a small bag of sand. They will gain an appreciation for the meaning, beauty, and utility of Navajo sand paintings.

## Processes/Skills

- Observing
- Using a hand lens
- Estimating
- Describing
- Comparing
- Counting
- Measuring
- Weighing
- Inferring
- Analyzing
- Recognizing shapes and patterns
- Problem solving
- Inquiring
- Designing
- Creating

- Reflecting
- Communicating

## Recommended For

*Grades 5–8: Individual and small-group instruction*
Adapt the lesson for fifth graders by preprinting the sand painting sketches in Procedure 6, offering several options to the students. You can also offer more help with the estimation problems.

## Time Required

2–3 hours

## Materials Required for Main Activity

- Sand
- Hand lenses
- Photos of Navajo sand paintings (or actual sand paintings)
- Paper
- Glue sticks
- Food coloring
- Newspaper
- Scales or balances

## Connecting to the Standards

### NSES
**Grade 5–8 Content Standards:**
Standard A: Science as Inquiry

- Abilities necessary to do scientific inquiry (especially observing carefully, thinking critically about evidence to develop and communicate good explanations, and using mathematics effectively)
- Understanding about scientific inquiry (especially emphasizing the value of evidence and mathematics)

Standard D: Earth Science

- Structure of the Earth system (especially regarding the properties of sand and soil)

## NCTM
**Standards for Grades 3–8:**

- Numbers and Operations (especially using numbers and operations to solve problems, developing an understanding of large numbers, and developing strategies to estimate large numbers)

- Problem Solving (especially using problem solving to build new math knowledge)

## Safety Considerations
Basic classroom safety practices apply.

## Activity Objectives
In this activity, students

- observe, describe, and compare sand grains;

- estimate the number of sand grains on their paintings (area) and in a small container displayed by the teacher (volume), thus contrasting area and volume; and

- create, observe, compare, and reflect on Navajo-style sand paintings.

## Background Information
Traditionally, Navajo sand paintings are used in healing and other important spiritual rituals. They are often used in conjunction with prayers, chants, and dances in ceremonies that may last several days. The paintings represent the supernatural spirits and invoke the power of those beings. Sand paintings are made directly on the earth and are swept up soon after completion. Their size ranges from 4 to 18 feet wide, and their shape can be square, oblong, or round. They often incorporate the four cardinal directions (east, white; south, yellow; west, blue; north, black). The pigments are taken from the earth: white from rock, red and yellow from ochre, black from charcoal mixed with sand, blue/gray from a mixture of white and black, and pink from red and white.

# Main Activity, Step-by-Step Procedures

1.  Ask students, "What is sand?" Brainstorm answers as a class or in small groups. Encourage a variety of responses, documenting them all on the chalkboard. Then ask students, "How could we find out more about sand? What are some things we could do with sand? What would you like to know about sand?" Again, encourage a variety of responses, first by having students record their responses in their science journals, then by offering their ideas publicly, in small groups.

2.  For each group of students, provide a small dish or plastic bag of sand, some newspapers or paper towels, and a hand lens. Also helpful, but not necessary, would be a small flashlight as an aid in viewing sand under the lens. Ask students, "How many grains of sand do you think are in this bag/dish? How did you decide on that number? What are some other ways to estimate?" Allow sufficient time for the groups to consider the questions. As students report, record on the chalkboard their rough estimations and brainstormed techniques for estimating.

3.  Now conduct general research on the sand samples. Challenge student groups to learn as much as they can about the sand. No observation should be considered too big or too small. All observations must be recorded on a data sheet or in a science journal. Students can also compare the sand to a small sample of more typical soil, potting soil, clay, and/or other such substances. Groups should share all their research findings in a classwide "symposium" or "scientific conference" on sand. Again ask, "What else would you like to know about sand?" Students' responses could form the basis for extension activities to be conducted later.

4.  Show photos of Navajo sand paintings, or actual sand paintings if you have them or can find them on the internet (see Figure 13.1 for several design examples). Ask, "What do the paintings have in common? Why do you suppose that the artists chose these designs? What other art forms are the Navajo known for (e.g., woven rugs, silver jewelry, ceramics)? What designs would you make in a sand painting?" During the discussion of the sand paintings, you can share information about the Navajo people and their arts, perhaps discovered during an internet search. Find out what other questions students have about the Navajo. Here is an opportunity for inquiry-based research on the tribe's history, sociology, geography, art, philosophy, and general way of life.

**FIGURE 13.1.** Navajo designs

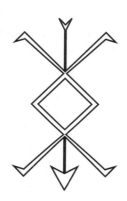

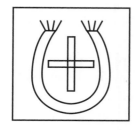
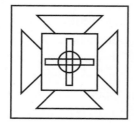
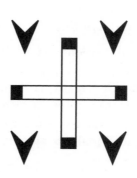

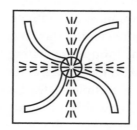

**SCIENCE**
Understanding about
scientific inquiry

5.  Next, students will have a chance to make their own sand paintings. Although Navajo sand paintings were traditionally made on the ground with loose sand, using no glue or other fixative, students can make a more permanent product on paper. You'll need to color the sand ahead of time by soaking plain sand in water tinted with food coloring for an hour, pouring off the water, and letting the sand dry overnight. The basic technique for making the sand painting itself is this: On a piece of clean white paper, sketch the desired design lightly in pencil, apply glue to a portion of the painting, sprinkle with sand, shake off the excess sand, apply glue and sand to another area, and so on until the piece is completed.

6.  Provide students with materials (paper, glue sticks, various colors of sand, newspaper to cover the work surface) and let them create their own sand paintings.

7.  When all students have completed their projects, analyze the sand-painting process (what worked, what didn't work, what problems they had, what surprises occurred, what they enjoyed) and allow each group to present its work. Discuss or write about reactions to the various sand paintings. Ask students, "How are the paintings like traditional Navajo art? How are they different?"

8.  Now it's time to estimate the number of sand grains in a given area or volume. As an introduction, ask students, "When have you wanted to know the approximate number of a large number of objects? Can you think of any situations where people might want to estimate amounts or numbers?" Encourage variety in responses; you may want to offer a "warm-up" example or two (e.g., How much pet food would you need to leave behind if you went away on a week-long trip?). Challenge students to estimate the number of sand grains on their sand paintings. Resist the temptation to offer specific hints; let them work it out in groups, but do make sure that they have access to hand lenses, rulers, and scales or balances. They *could* estimate the sand grains on a painting by counting the grains within a small area (e.g., one square centimeter) and multiplying by the estimated number of square centimeters covered in sand on the entire painting. If the working groups are getting too frustrated, you can gently encourage them with hints to send them in this direction. The less you suggest in terms of technique, the better. When the time is right, ask groups to explain how they proceeded to solve this problem. Ask them to reflect on the process: "Which techniques were effective? Why? Which weren't? Why? How do these estimations compare with those made

earlier (in Procedure 2)?" Point out that the first problem (Procedure 2) was an estimate involving volume (height × width × depth; three-dimensional space) and the second (Procedure 8) was an estimate involving area (height × width; two-dimensional surface).

9. Now revisit the question posed in Procedure 2; challenge students to estimate the number of grains in the bag, dish, or other container, after considering the methods used in the sand-painting estimations. Provide each group with a similar container of sand. Again, let the groups work through the answer on their own. If, after a time, students are too frustrated, you can offer hints leading to any of several solutions: counting the number of grains in a pinch or a small spoonful (unit of volume) and multiplying, or weighing (mass) a pinch or small spoonful and counting its grains, then multiplying, etc. The idea here is to encourage the development of problem-solving skills and to allow students to "own" their solutions, possibly using you, the teacher, as a resource person. When the task is completed, analyze and reflect on the various methods used. Conclude by asking how estimation could be usefully applied to students' own lives.

## Discussion Questions

Ask students the following:

1. How are sand grains similar to one another? How are they different? How does sand compare with potting soil? What have you learned about sand?

2. Can you think of a situation in which you or someone else might need to estimate a large quantity of sand or other substance?

3. How is *estimating* like *counting?* How is it different?

4. Can you think of ways in which *area* and *volume* are alike? Ways in which they are different?

5. Why do you think that sand paintings are important to the Navajo people? What else would you like to find out about the Navajo?

## Assessment

Suggestions for specific ways to assess student understanding are provided in parentheses.

1. Were students able to successfully observe and describe sand grains and to compare them with other soil-type substances? (Use

observations made during Procedure 3 as a performance assessment, and use Discussion Questions 1 and 2 as embedded assessments or as writing prompts for a science journal entry.)

2. Were students able to estimate the number of sand grains in area and in volume? Did they explore several methods of estimation, choosing (with or without teacher facilitation) the most effective technique(s)? (Use observations made during Procedures 2, 8, and 9 as performance assessments, and use Discussion Questions 3 and 4 as embedded evidence or as writing prompts for science journal entries.)

3. Did students create, observe, and compare Navajo-style sand paintings? (Use observations made during Procedures 5–7 as performance assessments, and use Discussion Question 5 as an embedded assessment or as a writing prompt for science journal entries.)

## RUBRIC 13.1
### Sample rubric using these assessment options

| | Achievement Level | | |
| --- | --- | --- | --- |
| | Developing 1 | Proficient 2 | Exemplary 3 |
| Were students able to successfully observe and describe sand grains and to compare them with other soil-type substances? | Observed, but unsuccessfully described and/or compared, sand grains | Successfully observed and described sand grains, but unsuccessfully compared with other substances | Successfully observed and described sand grains and effectively compared them with other substances |
| Were students able to estimate the number of sand grains in area and in volume? Did they explore several methods of estimation, choosing (with or without teacher facilitation) the most effective technique(s)? | Attempted to estimate the number of sand grains but were not successful | Successfully estimated the number of sand grains in both area and volume but did not explore a variety of estimation methods | Successfully estimated the number of sand grains in both area and volume and explored several estimation methods that they could discuss in some detail |
| Did students create, observe, and compare Navajo-style sand paintings? | Attempted to create, observe, and compare sand paintings but unsuccessfully | Successfully created and observed sand paintings but made few or no comparisons | Successfully created, observed, and compared sand paintings |

## Other Options and Extensions

1. Homework: Ask students to go home and estimate at least three large amounts; these could be in the actual home or somewhere in the community—consider rice grains or dried peas in a small plastic

container or blades of grass in a $10^2$ cm piece of lawn. This assignment can be done with family members.

**2.** Have students conduct research on sand paintings in other cultures, such as Tibetan mandalas. They can find photos or illustrations on the internet or in the library and make one of the paintings on their own.

**3.** Have the entire class produce a mural-sized sand painting, or a sand painting–style mural.

**4.** Have students make sand paintings using geometric designs only (e.g., angles, shapes, repeating patterns), and then ask them to describe their work in geometric and mathematical terms.

## Resources

Alexander, D. 1994. The dirt finders. *Science and Children* 31 (7): 12–14.

Carp, K. S. 1994. Telling tales: Creating graphs using multicultural literature. *Teaching Children Mathematics* 1: 87–91.

Lang, F. K. 2001. What is a "good guess" anyway? *Teaching Children Mathematics* 7 (8): 462.

Stroud, S. 1980. An affair with sand. *Science and Children* 18 (2): 22–25.

Underhill, R. M. 1965. *Red man's religion: Beliefs and practices of the Indians north of Mexico.* Chicago: University of Chicago Press.

Varelas, M., and J. Benhart. 2004. Welcome to rock day. *Science and Children* 41 (4): 40–45.

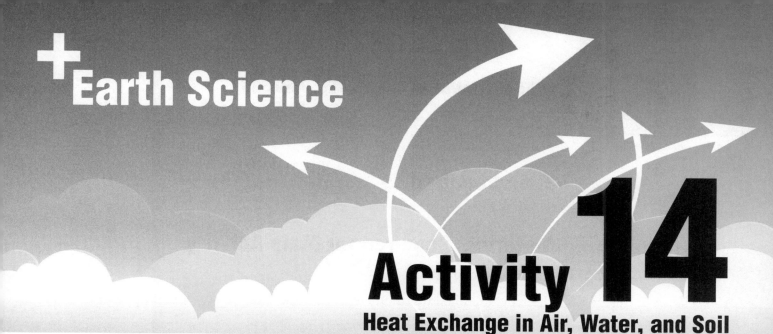

# Earth Science

# Activity 14
## Heat Exchange in Air, Water, and Soil

## Overview

The Earth is composed, at least at the surface, of soil/rock, water, and air. How do the heat exchange properties of these three very different substances compare, and what effect, if any, do they have on climate and weather? This activity represents a somewhat more advanced investigation of a complex subject, but is readily adapted to lower grades.

## Processes/Skills

- Observing
- Inquiring
- Describing
- Counting
- Measuring
- Graphing
- Analyzing data
- Problem solving
- Concluding
- Applying conclusions
- Communicating

## Recommended For

*Grades 6–8: Small-group or whole-class instruction*
You can adapt the activity for grade 6 by conducting the investigation as a whole-class exercise, rather than in small groups.

## Time Required

1–2 hours

## Materials Required for Main Activity

- Plastic cups (large size)
- Alcohol-filled thermometers or temperature probes for computer or graphing calculator
- Soil (or sand)
- Water
- Desk lamp(s)
- Graph paper

## Connecting to the Standards

### NSES
**Grade 5–8 Content Standards:**

Standard A: Science as Inquiry

- Abilities necessary to do scientific inquiry (especially observing carefully, thinking critically about evidence to develop and communicate good explanations, and using mathematics effectively)
- Understanding about scientific inquiry (especially emphasizing the value of evidence and mathematics)

Standard D: Earth Science

- Structure of the Earth system (especially regarding the properties of soil, water, and air)
- Transfer of energy (especially that heat moves in predictable ways)

### NCTM
**Standards for Grades 3–8:**

- Measurement (especially understanding and applying the metric system)
- Data Analysis and Probability (especially displaying relevant data to answer questions)
- Reasoning and Proof (especially engaging in thinking and reasoning)

- Connections (especially recognizing the connections among mathematical ideas and to investigations outside mathematics)

## Safety Considerations

Basic classroom safety practices apply. If you use alcohol-filled thermometers (do not use mercury-filled thermometers), be sure to choose those with metal safety backs.

## Activity Objectives

In this activity, students

- explore the heat exchange properties of the three substances (air, soil, water);

- make thoughtful connections between heat exchange and climate/weather patterns; and

- collect, display, and analyze their numerical data regarding heat exchange.

## Main Activity, Step-by-Step Procedures

1. Ask students to recall a time when they sat outside in the sunlight—maybe at the beach or at a local park. Better yet, if it is in fact a sunny day, go outside and let everyone stand in the sunlight for a few minutes. Ask students how they would describe their experiences, especially in terms of temperature changes. They will probably say that they became warm. This is an example of *heat exchange*, in particular *heat conduction*, which is when heat flows from one object or substance (in this case, the air) to another (in this case, the students themselves). What do the students do when they become too warm? They leave the sunlight and somehow find shelter. But the Sun shines 24 hours a day, 7 days a week, and the Earth itself cannot find shelter from the Sun's light and warmth. Explore the following questions with the class: How do the substances of the Earth (air, soil, water) react to the warmth of the Sun? Are they all the same, or do they react differently? Do they differ in how they conduct heat? Do some of the Earth's substances retain heat better than others (that is, do some substances lose, or *radiate*, heat more slowly than others)? How could we find out? Encourage diverse responses and try the ideas. One particular means of inquiry follows.

2. Divide the class into three groups (or multiples of three), one for each of the three substances mentioned. Provide each group with a

**SCIENCE**
Structure of the Earth system
Transfer of energy

## HEAT EXCHANGE IN AIR, WATER, AND SOIL

## STANDARDS

### SCIENCE
Understanding about
scientific inquiry

### MATH
Data analysis and
probability
Reasoning and proof
Connections

large plastic cup filled with a single substance, that is, either a cup of air, soil (or sand), or water. Each group also receives a thermometer, which is placed into the central portion of their substances. Students should predict which substances will heat fastest and which will lose heat the fastest. That is, which substances will conduct and radiate heat most quickly? Students should be sure that all substances are initially at room temperature, and record that temperature. Students immediately place each of the three cups directly under identical desk lamps and record each substance's temperature every minute for 15 minutes, using Activity Sheet 14.1, p. 149, to record data. At the end of that 15-minute period, students turn off the lamps and continue recording temperature readings each minute for the next 15 minutes. Results will vary significantly depending on how deeply the thermometer is inserted into the soil/sand and on how close the three substances are to the lamp, so all groups should try to be consistent.

3. All groups then share data so that everyone has results for all three of the substances. In the last column of the data table (Activity Sheet 14.1) students can calculate the heat retained, if any, by each of the substances. (Find the difference between Minute 15 Temperature and Minute 30 Temperature.) Ask students how else they could decide which substance retains heat best, worst, and so on. Suggest they plot temperature ($y$ axis) versus time ($x$ axis) for all three substances on a single graph so that they can be easily compared throughout the 30-minute time period. (Each of the three resulting lines should be labeled so that students can tell them apart.)

4. Ask students, "According to the graph, which substance warmed the fastest? Which cooled the quickest? How do you know? Which substance retained heat most effectively? That is, which lost its heat most slowly? How close were your predictions to the actual results?" For more advanced students, the inquiry can expand into actual rates of heat gain and loss in degrees per minute.

5. Ideally, water generally retains heat most efficiently, followed by soil (or sand), and air. Water retains heat well and acts like a heat reservoir: It heats slowly and cools slowly. Explain that heat is conducted, but cold is not. Air, like most gases, is a poor conductor of heat because it has few molecules per unit of volume with which to transfer heat energy. Air (and water) can transport heat effectively via *convection*, however. Convection refers to the transport of heat energy by the actual motion of the heated gas (or liquid). Currents caused by convection are easily seen in boiling water. Solid land

(e.g., rock, clay, sand, and soil) conducts and radiates heat efficiently, allowing it to heat *and* cool quickly. Heat exchange in real systems is quite complex because it is influenced by many variables, including mass, evaporation, and reflectivity of the substances being heated.

6. Explain that the interplay among the temperature differentials of atmosphere, water (especially oceans), and land (especially continents) has a huge impact on the climate, weather, and the general circulation of the Earth's atmosphere. For instance, in coastal areas during the day, the land tends to be warmer than the adjacent ocean, and the opposite is true at night. This effect tends to stabilize the region's temperature and often causes daytime onshore breezes and nighttime offshore breezes, which affect the level of comfort for residents. On the other hand, continental heartlands, far from the influence of sea or ocean, tend to be very hot in the summer and very cold in the winter.

## Discussion Questions
Ask students the following:

1. How do the thermal properties of air, soil, and water affect climate and/or weather?

2. How did mathematics help you determine the differences in heat exchange of the three substances (air, soil, water)? Could you have reached a meaningful conclusion without using math?

3. Why do some people want to live near an ocean or sea, in terms of the water source's effect on weather/climate? Would you like to live in this type of climate? Why or why not?

## Assessment
Suggestions for specific ways to assess student understanding are provided in parentheses.

1. Did students successfully explore the heat exchange properties of the three substances (air, soil, water)? (Use observations made during Procedure 2 as a performance assessment, and use Discussion Question 1 as an embedded evidence or as a writing prompt for a science journal entry.)

2. Were students able to make thoughtful connections between heat exchange and climate and/or weather patterns? (Use Discussion Question 3 as an embedded assessment or as a writing prompt for a science journal entry.)

3. Could students successfully collect, display, and analyze their numerical data regarding heat exchange? (Use observations made during Procedure 3 and Activity Sheet 14.1 as performance assessments, and use Discussion Question 2 as an embedded assessment or as a writing prompt for a science journal entry.)

**RUBRIC 14.1**
**Sample rubric using these assessment options**

| | Achievement Level | | |
|---|---|---|---|
| | **Developing**<br>**1** | **Proficient**<br>**2** | **Exemplary**<br>**3** |
| Did students successfully explore the heat exchange properties of the three substances (air, soil, water)? | Attempted to explore heat exchange but were not particularly successful | Successfully explored heat exchange | Successfully explored heat exchange and could explain their investigation in detail using appropriate terminology |
| Were students able to make thoughtful connections between heat exchange and climate/weather patterns? | Attempted to describe the connections but were not successful to any significant extent | Successfully described the basic connections between heat exchange and some climate/weather patterns | Successfully described in considerable detail, using appropriate terminology, the connections between heat exchange and some climate/weather patterns |
| Could students successfully collect, display, and analyze their numerical data regarding heat exchange? | Collected their data but were unsuccessful in displaying and analyzing it | Successfully collected, displayed, and analyzed their data | Successfully collected, displayed, and analyzed their data and could explain the process in detail using appropriate terminology |

# Other Options and Extensions

1. Have students design and build model houses of different substances (clay, cardboard, paper, etc.). Instruct them to test the heat retention of the houses, using a lamp as a heat source. Students should record the temperature data and find out which home material insulates best. Students also can test different designs for thermal differences.

2. Give each student group an ice cube (in the bottom of a clear plastic cup so that it is visible and you can see when it has melted) and challenge them to insulate the cube so that it lasts as long as possible under a desk lamp. Offer a variety of materials (cotton, paper, cardboard, packing bubbles, etc.) to place over the cube for insulation against the heat of the lamp.

**3.** Have students test the thermal properties of saltwater (using the basic procedure in Step 2), and compare the thermal properties of saltwater to those of freshwater. Students can compare the thermal properties of different types of soil and/or compare moist air (putting a damp paper towel in the bottom of the cup) with dry air for heat gain and loss.

## Resources

Buczynski, S. 2006. What's hot? What's not? *Science and Children* 44 (2): 25–29.

Cavallo, A. M. I. 2001. Convection connections. *Science and Children* 38 (8): 20–25.

Chick, L., A. S. Holmes, N. McClymonds, S. Musick, P. Reynolds, and P. Shultz. 2008. Weather or not. *Teaching Children Mathematics* 14 (8): 464–465.

Critchfield, H. J. 1983. *General climatology.* Englewood Cliffs, NJ: Prentice-Hall.

Gates, D. M. 1972. *Man and his environment: Climate.* New York: Harper and Row.

Heating up, cooling down. 2005. *Science and Children* 42 (8): 47–48.

Pearlman, S., and K. Pericak-Spector. 1995. Graph that data. *Science and Children* 32 (4): 35–37.

Whitin, D. J., and P. Whitin. 2003. Talk counts: Discussing graphs with young children. *Teaching Children Mathematics* 10 (3): 142–149.

## ACTIVITY SHEET 14.1
## Heat Exchange in Air, Water, and Soil

Predict: Rank order the three substances (air, soil, water) in terms of how well you think they will be able to retain heat.

| Ranking | Prediction | Actual |
|---|---|---|
| Most Effective | | |
| Second Most Effective | | |
| Least Effective | | |

Record heat gain (conduction) and heat loss (radiation) data for all three substances. Each group will experiment with a single substance.

Room temperature (initial temperature of all three substances) = _____ °C

**EARTH SCIENCE**

**Data Table**

| | Lamp on (First 15 Minutes; Record Temperature) | | | | | | | | | | | | | | | Lamp off (Last 15 Minutes; Record Temperature) | | | | | | | | | | | | | | | HR* |
|---|---|---|---|---|---|---|---|---|---|---|---|---|---|---|---|---|---|---|---|---|---|---|---|---|---|---|---|---|---|---|---|
| | 1 | 2 | 3 | 4 | 5 | 6 | 7 | 8 | 9 | 10 | 11 | 12 | 13 | 14 | 15 | 16 | 17 | 18 | 19 | 20 | 21 | 22 | 23 | 24 | 25 | 26 | 27 | 28 | 29 | 30 | |
| Air | | | | | | | | | | | | | | | | | | | | | | | | | | | | | | | |
| Soil | | | | | | | | | | | | | | | | | | | | | | | | | | | | | | | |
| Water | | | | | | | | | | | | | | | | | | | | | | | | | | | | | | | |

* HR (Heat Retained): Minute 15 Temperature minus Minute 30 Temperature

Graph the class data for all three substances: time ($x$ axis) versus temperature ($y$ axis). What can you conclude based on the data?

# + Earth Science

# Activity 15

## Developing a Model of the Earth's Inner Structure

## Overview

How much do your students know about the Earth's interior? This activity will provide them with a hands-on experience, as well as with appropriate terms and concepts. Students discover what makes a good model as they first choose a fruit or vegetable model and then create a two-dimensional, and possibly a three-dimensional, clay model of the Earth's interior. They will use proportion and estimation to build their clay models. They also will compare their various models for accuracy and overall utility.

## Processes/Skills

- Observing
- Creating
- Describing
- Estimating
- Analyzing
- Measuring
- Calculating
- Communicating
- Reasoning
- Recognizing patterns
- Problem solving
- Developing spatial sense
- Cooperating

# DEVELOPING A MODEL OF THE EARTH'S INNER STRUCTURE

## Recommended For

*Grades 5–8: Small-group instruction*
You can adjust for fifth graders by doing the proportion problem in Procedure 4 as a whole class.

## Time Required

1–2 hours

## Materials Required for Main Activity

- A variety of fruits and vegetables (peach or nectarine, avocado, potato, orange, apple, grape, tomato)
- Paper
- Drawing compasses
- Calculators
- Clay (three different colors)
- Balances

## Connecting to the Standards

### NSES
**Grade 5–8 Content Standards:**
Standard A: Science as Inquiry

- Abilities necessary to do scientific inquiry (especially observing carefully, thinking critically about evidence to develop and communicate good explanations, and using mathematics effectively)
- Understanding about scientific inquiry (especially recognizing the importance of mathematics in science and noticing that scientific explanations emphasize evidence and logically consistent arguments)

Standard D: Earth Science

- Structure of the Earth system (especially regarding the structure of the Earth's lithosphere, mantle, and core)

### NCTM
**Standards for Grades 3–8:**

- Numbers and Operations (especially using numbers and operations to solve problems)

- Geometry (especially comparing three-dimensional shapes)
- Problem Solving (especially applying strategies to solve problems)
- Reasoning and Proof (especially engaging in thinking and reasoning)

## Safety Considerations

Basic classroom safety practices apply. The fruits and vegetables used in this activity should not be eaten in the classroom during or after this investigation.

## Activity Objectives

In this activity, students

- choose good fruit or vegetable models of the Earth and explain their reasoning;

- construct accurate clay models of the Earth, calculating or estimating the amount of clay needed for each layer; and

- compare and analyze their various models of the Earth's inner structure.

## Background Information

The Earth is composed of three layers (see Figure 15.1). The *core* has an inner solid portion surrounded by a liquid portion. The *mantle* is mostly solid rock, but also contains *magma*, or molten rock. The rocks of the *crust* create the continents and the ocean floors. The Earth's materials have been distributed based on their *density*, with the heavier materials found near the planet's center (the core being composed mostly of nickel and iron) and the lighter materials in the crust. The deepest that humans have bored into the Earth is at a geological test site in Siberia (more than 12.2 km deep). Most of what we know about the composition of the inner Earth is based on studies of *seismic waves* (i.e., earthquake waves moving through rocks and monitored by laboratory instruments as they travel through the various layers of the planet). The deeper you go into the Earth, the warmer the temperature becomes. The heat comes from the original heat that was generated when the planet was formed and from *radioactivity*. *Plate tectonics* refers to

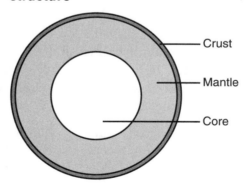

**FIGURE 15.1. Earth's inner structure**

Crust

Mantle

Core

# DEVELOPING A MODEL OF THE EARTH'S INNER STRUCTURE

SCIENCE
Structure of the Earth
  system

SCIENCE
Abilities necessary to do
  scientific inquiry

MATH
Numbers and operations
Geometry
Problem solving

the movement of the "plates" in the crust, driven by convection of the mantle (the plates are pushed by the hot, shifting mantle underneath). The crust's plates are constantly, but very slowly (because the plates usually move only a few centimeters each year), being created and destroyed. Where plates diverge, new crust is created as magma rises from the mantle. Where plates diverge, the leading edge of the crustal plate is pushed down and lost into the underlying mantle. Most *earthquakes* occur along the boundaries of tectonic plates as the plates slide against one another.

## Main Activity, Step-by-Step Procedures

1.  Begin with a simple question: "What do you know about the inner structure of the Earth? That is, what is the Earth like on the inside?" Encourage a wide variety of responses. Offer student groups a variety of types of fruits and vegetables (peach or nectarine, avocado, potato, orange, apple, grape, tomato, etc.) and ask them to choose the one that they think best represents the structure of the Earth, especially considering what the planet is like on the inside. Be sure that they know they will be responsible for explaining their reasoning. Provide students with enough time to complete the task.

2.  Ask each student group to present its fruit or vegetable choice and rationale. Because their explanations will be based on very limited knowledge, ask what they need to know about the Earth to really pick the best piece of produce as an Earth model. List their responses on the board. They should want to know more about what the inside of the Earth is like.

    During and after students' fruit/vegetable model presentations, explain the basics about the internal composition of the planet Earth. Include the basic cross section (Figure 15.1) of core, mantle, and crust. This conceptual information is found in the Background Information section.

3.  Ask again which produce item is the best model of the Earth, based on students' new understanding of the facts. Ask groups to explain their answers in light of the information about the Earth's inner structure. Did they choose a different produce item this time? Why or why not?

    Have each student draw a cross section of the Earth, labeling the core, mantle, and crust. Point out that this cross-sectional model is done in two dimensions (height and width). Also explain that students should base their drawings on the approximate thicknesses of each

layer, which are as follows: core = 3,400 km; mantle = 2,900 km; crust = 50 km.

4. Ask students, "If you were going to make a flat, cross-sectional model of the Earth with a diameter of 10 cm, made from three different colors of clay (core = blue, mantle = red, crust = green), how much of each color would you need? That is, would you need more blue, red, or green, and can you decide just how much you would need to make your 'model Earth' in cross section?" For older or more advanced students, the answers can be found using the thicknesses of the Earth's layers to calculate the proportions of clay, in grams, needed for the model. (They'll need to consider the relative proportions of the three layers, based on the layer's diameters, and then use those proportions to determine the relative amounts of clay, in grams, needed for the model.) If you want to add an extra challenge, ask students to make a hemispheric (i.e., three-dimensional, as opposed to the two-dimensional cross section) model with an overall diameter of 10 cm. (Encourage divergent solutions to the problem, which should involve not only the relative proportions of the three layers, but also a determination of the mass of a 10 cm clay sphere, which must then be partitioned into the three colors.) Younger students can simply estimate the approximate proportions of the three layers. Be sure that each group can explain its rationale.

5. As the student groups complete their calculations and/or estimates, offer clay and balances so that they can weigh out the proper amounts of each color and build their models. Groups can then compare and analyze their models for accuracy. Finally, ask students to determine and explain which is a better model of the Earth's structure: the clay cross section or the piece of produce? Consider the sort of information each model offers, which model is most like the actual Earth, whether the model is practical (too small, too large, etc.), and any other considerations that come to mind.

**SCIENCE**
Understanding about scientific inquiry

**MATH**
Reasoning and proof

## Discussion Questions

Ask students the following:

1. Which fruit or vegetable was most like the Earth? Which was least like the Earth? How do you know? Can you think of another fruit or vegetable that would make a better model of the Earth? Explain your answer.

2.  How did your group determine the amount of each color of clay needed for your three-dimensional model of the Earth?

3.  How is your clay model like the Earth? How is it different?

4.  What makes something a good model of something else? What are some things to consider when making a model of something?

## Assessment

Suggestions for specific ways to assess student understanding are provided in parentheses.

1.  Were students able to choose a good fruit or vegetable model of the Earth and explain their reasoning? (Use observations made during Procedure 3 as a performance assessment, and use Discussion Question 1 as embedded evidence or as a writing prompt for a science journal entry.)

2.  Were students able to construct accurate clay models of the Earth, calculating or estimating the amount of clay needed for each layer? (Use observations made during Procedure 4 as a performance assessment, and use Discussion Question 2 as embedded evidence or as a writing prompt for a science journal entry.)

3.  Could students compare and analyze the different Earth models, explaining what makes the difference between a good and a bad model? (Use Discussion Questions 3 and 4 as embedded assessments or as writing prompts for science journal entries.)

**RUBRIC 15.1**
**Sample rubric using these assessment options**

| | Achievement Level | | |
| --- | --- | --- | --- |
| | Developing 1 | Proficient 2 | Exemplary 3 |
| Were students able to choose a good fruit or vegetable model of the Earth and explain their reasoning? | Unsuccessfully attempted to choose a good model | Chose a good model and gave a basic explanation of how they made that choice | Chose a good model and gave a detailed explanation, including the use of appropriate terminology |
| Were students able to construct accurate clay models of the Earth, calculating or estimating the amount of clay needed for each layer? | Unsuccessfully attempted to construct a clay model | Successfully constructed a model and were able to calculate or estimate an accurate amount of clay for each layer | Successfully constructed a model, were able to calculate or estimate an accurate amount of clay for each layer, and were able to explain the process in detail |
| Could students compare and analyze the different Earth models, explaining what makes the difference between a good and a bad model? | Attempted to compare the models but were not successful to any significant extent | Successfully compared the models and explained the basic difference between good and bad models | Successfully compared the models and explained the difference between good and bad models in detail, using appropriate terminology and offering several examples |

# Other Options and Extensions

1. Encourage students to find out more about the interior of the Earth through research, either in the library or via the internet. They can discover answers to their own questions.

2. Have advanced students determine the scale of the clay Earth model.

3. Have students make models of other planets (based on their research of size and interior structure) and compare them to their Earth models.

## Resources

Gabel, D. L., ed. 1994. *Handbook of research on science teaching and learning*. New York: Macmillan.
Gaylen, N. 1998. Encouraging curiosity at home. *Science and Children* 35 (4): 24–25.
Kelly, C. 2002. The diminishing apple. *Science and Children* 39 (5): 26–30.

Lightman, A., and P. Sadler. 1988. The Earth is round? Who are you kidding? *Science and Children* 25 (5): 24–26.

Trefil, J. 1992. *1001 things everyone should know about science*. New York: Doubleday.

Yang, D. 2006. Developing number sense through real-life situations in school. *Teaching Children Mathematics* 13 (2): 104–106.

# Activity 16
## Determining the Size and Shape of the Blind Spot

## Overview

What exactly is the blind spot? It is the place where the optic nerve meets the back of the retina (see Figure 16.1, p. 161). Because no sensory cells are present in the retina at the meeting point, a "hole" is created in the field of view of each eye. The brain "fills in" the hole with what "ought" to be there, so we usually don't notice the blind spots. In this activity, students will determine several characteristics of the visual blind spot, including its approximate size and shape, as well as its impact on daily life. This lesson will tie in nicely with Activities 6, 7, and 17.

## Processes/Skills

- Observing
- Comparing
- Describing
- Making conclusions
- Experimenting
- Identifying shapes and patterns
- Predicting
- Estimating
- Measuring
- Calculating
- Applying
- Communicating
- Developing spatial reasoning
- Inquiring
- Cooperating

## Recommended For

*Grades 5–8: Small-group instruction*
You can adapt the activity for grades 5 and 6 by conducting the investigation as a whole-class exercise, rather than in small groups.

## Time Required

2–3 hours

## Materials Required for Main Activity

- Paper
- Pencils or fine-point marking pens
- Metric rulers
- The classroom chalkboard
- Chalk
- Calculators (optional)

## Connecting to the Standards

### NSES
### Grade 5–8 Content Standards:
Standard A: Science as Inquiry

- Abilities necessary to do scientific inquiry (especially observing carefully, thinking critically about evidence to develop and communicate good explanations, and using mathematics effectively)

- Understanding about scientific inquiry (especially recognizing the importance of mathematics in science and noticing that scientific explanations emphasize evidence and logically consistent arguments)

Standard C: Life Science

- Structure and function in living systems (especially that structure and function are complementary)

- Diversity and adaptations of organisms (especially regarding biological adaptations that enhance species survival)

## NCTM
**Standards for Grades 3–8:**

- Numbers and Operations (especially understanding operations and how they relate to one another)

- Algebra (especially using algebra to solve problems)

- Geometry (especially identifying, naming, and/or comparing two-dimensional shapes)

- Measurement (especially understanding and applying the metric system)

- Problem Solving (especially constructing new math knowledge through problem solving, and applying strategies to solve a mathematical problem)

- Connections (especially recognizing the connections among mathematical ideas and to investigations outside mathematics)

## Safety Considerations
Basic classroom safety practices apply.

## Activity Objectives
In this activity, students

- locate blind spots in both eyes;

- determine the approximate percentage of the entire field of view and the approximate shape of the blind spot; and

- explain the everyday implications, including the potential hazards, of having blind spots.

## Background Information
Let's look at the eye itself as an anatomical structure (see Figure 16.1). Light enters the eye through a hole called the *pupil*, which is protected by the clear *cornea*. The pupil is surrounded by the colored part of the eye, the *iris*, which adjusts the size of the pupil by growing larger or smaller. (You can demonstrate this by observing the eye of a partner as you carefully shine a small flashlight into his or her eye. The pupil shrinks, which means the iris expands,

**FIGURE16.1. The human eye (cross section)**

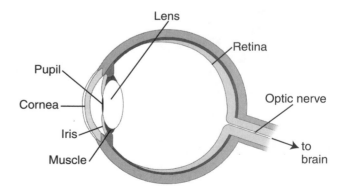

**DETERMINING THE SIZE AND SHAPE OF THE BLIND SPOT**

in bright light in order to control the amount of light entering the eye. The opposite effect can be noted in dim light. Enlargement of the pupils is called *dilation*, and shrinkage is called *contraction*.) The image passes through the lens and is focused by muscles that attach to the margins of the lens and control its shape. The image then falls onto the back surface of the eye, called the *retina*, producing a chemical message that transmits the image as a nerve impulse to the visual part of the brain via the optic nerve. The eyes, therefore, are really extensions of the brain and as such are considered part of the nervous system.

## Main Activity, Step-by-Step Procedures

1. Say to the class, "Did you know that you have a blind spot in each eye? Today we'll find it, determine its size, and determine its shape." Instruct pairs of students in the following procedure. "On a piece of paper, make a small X (about 1 cm long) with a marking pen, then make a dot (about 0.5 cm in diameter) about 5 cm to the right of the X (see Figure 16.2). Closing your left eye and holding the paper close to your face, focus on the X. Then slowly move the paper away from your face, still focused on the X, until the dot disappears from your peripheral vision. The dot should disappear at a distance of about 20 cm. Try this procedure a number of times so that you are very comfortable with locating your blind spot. Be sure that your partner can find his/her blind spot, too.

**FIGURE 16.2. Find your blind spot.**

If not, offer helpful suggestions. Can you find the blind spot in the left eye? How did you have to change the experimental setup?" (You must flip the dot to the left of the X, as opposed to the right.)

After students report their findings, explain the basic structure and function of the human eye, referring to Figure 16.1 (and the Background Information) as you proceed. Once they understand the fundamental structure of the eye, ask, "Can anyone explain *why* we have a blind spot in each eye, based on the eye's anatomy?" Encourage a variety of ideas, and assist students in recognizing that where the optic nerve meets the retina there are no sensory cells, forming a small blind spot. Ask students what questions they have about the blind spot.

**2.** Just how much of the field of view is taken up by the two blind spots? To estimate, first students will determine the approximate field of view, and then subtract the approximate size of the two blind spots from it. To determine the approximate field of view, students stand approximately 20 cm (or whatever distance you used to make the entire X disappear) from a chalkboard and look straight ahead. With a partner assisting, each student finds out how much of the chalkboard he or she can see at this distance (with eyes straight ahead) by marking the outer limits of what can be seen. The student should move a pencil to determine the points above, below, to the right, and to the left at which the pencil just moves into view. That is, he or she should mark the outer limits of the entire field of view at approximately 20 cm (or at whatever distance the entire X disappeared). These four points describe a rectangle, whose area the student can now determine. Using the approximate size of the blind spot, students can now calculate the approximate percentage of their entire fields of view that are taken up by their two blind spots (remember, there is a blind spot in each eye). Ask the class why this would be considered a rough approximation and not an accurate measurement.

**3.** What is the approximate shape of the blind spot? Students will modify the "X and dot" method a bit. They will use the same sort of dot, but instead of an X they'll try different shapes and see which ones are the easiest to make disappear. Have students try a square, a triangle, a rectangle, an oval, a circle, and any other shapes they think might fit. Ask, "Which do you predict will be closest to the shape of the blind spot?" Offer this hint: "Think of the cause of the blind spot: It occurs where the optic nerve meets the retina (see Figure 16.1), resulting in a small area with no optical sensory cells. What shape is the optic nerve? How might its shape affect the shape of the blind spot?"

**4.** Ask students, "How might the blind spot affect everyday life? Could we miss seeing things because of the blind spot? Is it possible that something as big as a person could fall within the blind spot so that we would be unable to see him or her?" Have students use the "X and dot" method from Step 1 to determine how tall an X they can "lose" at about 20 cm distance from their eyes. (They should start with a small X and continue making larger Xs until they find the tallest X that will fit entirely into the blind spot, keeping the distance of the paper with the X and dot constant at 20 cm throughout the

**MATH**
Numbers and Operations
Geometry
Measurement
Problem solving

**SCIENCE**
Structure and function in living systems

**SCIENCE**
Understanding about scientific inquiry

**MATH**
Algebra

**SCIENCE**
Diversity and adaptations
   of organisms

**MATH**
Connections

process.) Instruct students to use proportion to determine how far away a person would have to be to be able to be completely "lost" in the blind spot. That is, X (the approximate blind spot size, i.e., the size of the tallest X) divided by the constant distance (20 cm) equals human size divided by distance from the observer. (Consider human height to be 1.5 m.) This gives us an equation, X cm/20 cm = 1.5 m/unknown meters, where X cm is the tallest X determined via the "X and dot" method. Change all units into meters, and solve for the unknown distance in meters. That is approximately the distance at which a person can "disappear" into your blind spot.

5.   Ask, "Who should be concerned about the presence of their blind spots? (drivers, meat cutters, baseball players). How can a driver, for instance, surmount the problem of the blind spot?" Offer students the reminder that the blind spot is only a problem if the eyes are focused on a single point, so if you keep your eyes moving, you get a good view of the entire area in front of you. Drivers should remember this and keep their eyes moving around, looking here and there ahead of them, rather than just at a single part of the road ahead.

## Discussion Questions
Ask students the following:

1.   How much of your field of view is taken up by the blind spot? How do you know?

2.   What shape is the blind spot? How do you know?

3.   How might this blind spot be a problem for drivers? How else might it affect a person's life? How could the blind spot affect your life?

## Assessment
Suggestions for specific ways to assess student understanding are provided in parentheses.

1.   Were students able to successfully locate blind spots in each eye? (Use observations made during Procedure 1 as a performance assessment.)

2.   Were students able to determine the approximate percentage of the field of view that is taken up by the two blind spots? (Use observations made during Procedure 2 as a performance assessment, and use Discussion Question 1 as embedded evidence or as a writing prompt for a science journal entry.)

3. Were students able to come to a conclusion about the approximate shape of the blind spot? (Use observations made during Procedure 3 as a performance assessment, and use Discussion Question 2 as embedded evidence or as a writing prompt for a science journal entry.)

4. Could students calculate how far away a person would have to be to be able to become completely "lost" in his or her blind spot? (Use observations made during Procedure 4 as a performance assessment.)

5. Were students aware of the implications of the blind spot for everyday life? (Use Discussion Question 3 as an embedded assessment or as a writing prompt for a science journal entry.)

**RUBRIC 16.1**
**Sample rubric using these assessment options**

| | Achievement Level | | |
| | Developing 1 | Proficient 2 | Exemplary 3 |
|---|---|---|---|
| Were students able to successfully locate blind spots in each eye? | Attempted to locate the blind spots but were unsuccessful | Successfully located the blind spots | Successfully located the blind spots and were able to describe their work in detail using appropriate terminology |
| Were students able to determine the approximate percentage of the field of view that is taken up by the two blind spots? | Attempted to determine the size of the blind spot but were unsuccessful | Successfully determined the approximate size of the blind spots | Successfully determined the approximate size of the blind spots and were able to describe their work in detail using appropriate terminology |
| Were students able to come to a conclusion about the approximate shape of the blind spot? | Attempted to determine the shape of the blind spot but were unsuccessful | Successfully determined the shape of the blind spot | Successfully determined the shape of the blind spot and were able to describe their work in detail using appropriate terminology |
| Could students calculate how far away a person would have to be to be able to become completely "lost" in one's blind spot? | Attempted to calculate the distance but were unsuccessful | Successfully calculated the distance at which a person may be visually "lost" | Successfully calculated the distance at which a person may be visually "lost" and were able to describe their work in detail using appropriate terminology |
| Were students aware of the implications of the blind spot for everyday life? | Attempted to explain the implications but were not successful to any significant extent | Successfully explained the basic implications of the blind spot in daily life | Successfully explained, in detail and using appropriate terminology, the implications of the blind spot in daily life |

## Other Options and Extensions

1.  Ask students, "Do all vertebrates have blind spots, and if so, are they affected in any way? How can you find out?" Have them do research to find an answer.

2.  Have students dissect a vertebrate eye and observe the region of the blind spot. Ask students, "Does the blind spot look different from the surrounding retinal surface? If so, how?"

3.  Ask students to make a survey of adult drivers and find out how many of them are aware of the potential hazards associated with their blind spots. Students should share their findings with the class. Keep class records and discuss the implications of the survey.

4.  On the playground, show students how to make friends "disappear" by aligning them with their blind spots (see Main Activity, Step-by-Step Procedures, Step 4). Recommend that students use their findings from this activity, including the placement, shape, and size of the blind spot. Students should report their results to the class.

## Resources

Ostwald, T. 1995. An eye for learning. *Science and Children* 33 (2): 25–26.

Soares, J., M. L. Blanton, and J. J. Kaput. 2006. Thinking algebraically across the elementary school curriculum. *Teaching Children Mathematics* 12 (5): 228–235.

Walpole, B. 1988. *175 science experiments to amuse and amaze your friends*. New York: Random House.

# Life Science

# Activity 17
## Investigating Perception and Illusion

## Overview

For a motivating and baffling experience, try this investigation of perceptual illusions and their causes. It allows students to observe, analyze, and compare a variety of optical illusions, and also to create their own optical illusions with pencil, paint, and paper. Their results will lead them to make conclusions about visual perception and to generalize about broader aspects of sensory perception. In the process, students will discover that shapes play a major role in illusions and that it can be difficult for one individual to simultaneously maintain two different perspectives.

## Processes/Skills

- Observing
- Measuring
- Predicting
- Describing
- Inferring
- Recognizing mathematical relationships
- Communicating
- Recognizing patterns
- Problem solving
- Analyzing
- Inquiring
- Creating
- Cooperating

## Recommended For

*Grades 5–8: Small-group instruction*

Offer fifth graders plenty of support while they create their own optical illusions in Procedure 2.

## Time Required

1–2 hours

## Materials Required for Main Activity

- Illustrations of optical illusions (Figures 17.1 through 17.6, p. 171, or available from many different websites)
- General art supplies (paper, pens, pencils, paints)
- Drawing tools (erasers, protractors, drawing compasses)
- Transparency of Figure 17.7, p. 172 ("old lady/young lady")

## Materials Required for Going Further

- Transparency of Figure 17.8, p. 174 ("vase/faces")
- General art supplies (paper, pens, pencils, paints)

## Connecting to the Standards

### NSES
### Grade 5–8 Content Standards:

Standard A: Science as Inquiry

- Abilities necessary to do scientific inquiry (especially observing carefully, thinking critically about evidence to develop and communicate good explanations, and using mathematics effectively)
- Understanding about scientific inquiry (especially recognizing the importance of mathematics in science and noticing that scientific explanations emphasize evidence and logically consistent arguments)
- Diversity and adaptations of organisms (especially regarding biological adaptations that enhance species survival)

**NCTM**

**Standards for Grades 3–8:**

- Algebra (especially identifying and applying numeric and geometric patterns)

- Geometry (especially identifying, naming, and/or comparing two-dimensional shapes)

- Reasoning and Proof (especially engaging in thinking and reasoning)

## Safety Considerations

Basic classroom safety practices apply.

## Activity Objectives

In this activity, students

- explain the causes of some optical illusions and variances in visual perception;

- make and describe their own optical illusions; and

- identify arithmetic and geometric patterns associated with optical illusions.

## Main Activity, Step-by-Step Procedures

1.  Ask students what they know about optical illusions. You can record their responses in a brainstormed list on the chalkboard or on an overhead transparency for all to see. Ask, "Where have you seen optical illusions? What is it that you think creates an optical illusion?" Then ask the students, working in cooperative groups of two to four individuals, to observe the optical illusions illustrated in Figures 17.1 through 17.6. Student should analyze them, one by one, considering the following questions:

    a.  What is the illusion, as you see it? (Students should record the description in writing.)

    b.  What are the measurements of each illustration? (Students should keep written records of each measurement.)

    c.  How does what you perceive differ from what is actually there in each illusion?

    d.  What are differences and similarities between the various illusions? (Students should describe and record their ideas in writing.)

**SCIENCE**
Abilities necessary to do scientific inquiry

**MATH**
Algebra
Geometry

**INVESTIGATING PERCEPTION AND ILLUSION**

Try to identify patterns or repeating observations. Pay special attention to arithmetic and geometric patterns and relationships. For example, will Figure 17.2 still fool you if segments A and B are very long or very short? Will Figure 17.5 still fool you if each long segment has only one cross-hatched line instead of many?

**e.** What is the context or setting of each illusion? That is, how would you describe the foreground or the background? If you change the background or the foreground, will it alter your perception of the figure?

Lead a class discussion of the groups' findings. Ask, "Can you make any general statements about these optical illusions and how we perceive them?" Consider all possibilities and encourage divergent responses. These particular illusions are all the results of context or setting. For example, in Figure 17.1, circle A *contains* a square, whereas circle B is *set into* a square. This appears to "draw in" circle A and makes it appear smaller than circle B. In Figure 17.3, the center circle appears larger when placed within smaller circles, and smaller when placed within larger circles.

**2.** Next, direct students to create their own optical illusions. They may use Figures 17.1 through 17.6 as models, but if they do, encourage them to change some aspect(s) of the drawing to look for varying effects in perception. They might alter the illustration so that the illusion is even more pronounced, or they may want to design an entirely novel illusion. Either way, be sure that they have access to drawing tools: pencils, erasers, protractors, compasses, and so on. Encourage innovation, exploration, and "play."

Students can also add color to their illusions and investigate how color affects perception. An interesting experiment might be to design an illusion using only pencil and paper, and then to make an exact copy, except with color added. Does the addition of color change how a person perceives the illusion?

Discuss with your students what they now know or believe about optical illusions. After students have offered ideas, ask, "What creates such illusions? Can you recall seeing any optical illusions in real life?" Consider the apparent convergence of parallel railroad tracks, the apparently larger size of the full Moon when it's near the horizon as opposed to being high in the sky, and desert mirages. Explore how these real-life illusions are explained. This is an excellent opportunity for some student research.

**SCIENCE**
Understanding about
   scientific inquiry

**MATH**
Reasoning and proof

**LIFE SCIENCE**

**FIGURE 17.1.**
Which circle, A or B, is larger?

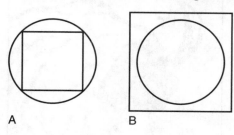

**FIGURE 17.2.**
Which line segment, A or B, is longest?

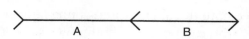

**FIGURE 17.3.**
Which is the larger center circle, A or B?

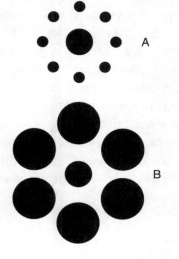

**FIGURE 17.4.**
Which inner angle is larger, A or B?

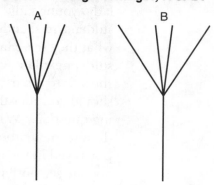

**FIGURE 17.5.**
Are any of the long lines parallel?
If so, which one(s)?

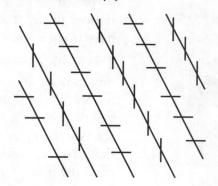

**FIGURE 17.6.**
Are either of the shapes perfect
squares? If so, which one(s)?

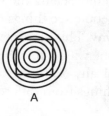

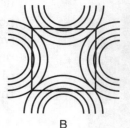

**INVESTIGATING PERCEPTION AND ILLUSION**

**3.** Show an overhead transparency of Figure 17.7 (the "old lady/young lady") and ask students to silently write down what they see. Have each student explain what he or she saw to a partner. Students should consider the following questions: Was there any disagreement about what was portrayed in the figure? Could anyone see both images? Did anyone have any difficulty seeing the second image? Could anyone see both images simultaneously? Were students surprised by this illusion? What surprised them about the experience? If any students can't see both the old lady and young lady, have them work with a partner who can point out both images.

**FIGURE 17.7. What do you see?**

The phenomenon being explored here is known as *perspective*, which means point of view. Whenever you observe anything, you examine it only from a single point of view, or perspective, at a time. An image of the old lady/young lady, for instance, strikes the retina and is sent via the optic nerve to the brain where it is interpreted (see Activity 16 for more information about how the eye works). The brain can only interpret the information one way at a time, however. That "one way" is called perspective. If you see the old lady, you can't simultaneously see the young lady, and vice versa. Your perspective can change from one to the other, though. Say to students, "How did you manage to change your perspective? That is, if you first saw the old lady, how did you change perspectives to see the young lady? Did anyone have any trouble seeing the second perspective? Difficulty seeing the second perspective is not uncommon. Often, when people see things one way they have a hard time seeing any other way. This also seems to be true of ideas. Once we interpret things one way, it may be difficult to see it any other way. Can you think of any examples of this in your life? How can we improve at seeing things from different perspectives?"

## Discussion Questions

Ask students the following:

**1.** Which of the illusions you've seen were most effective in fooling you? How do you explain their effectiveness? Did your classmates agree on the most effective illusions, or did different people have different perceptions of the various illusions?

**2.** Were you able to illustrate your own optical illusion? Was it an effective illusion? What would you do differently next time?

**3.** What arithmetic or geometric patterns were you able to identify in the various optical illusions?

**4.** Which did you see first: the old lady or the young lady? Were you able to see the other perspective? Was it difficult to see the other perspective, and, if so, how did you figure it out?

## Assessment

Suggestions for specific ways to assess student understanding are provided in parentheses.

**1.** Were students able to explain the causes of some optical illusions and variances in visual perception? (Use observations made during Procedure 1 as a performance assessment, and use Discussion Question 1 as embedded evidence or as a writing prompt for a science journal entry.)

**2.** Did students successfully make their own optical illusions for display? (Use observations made during Procedure 2 and student-created illusions as performance assessments, and use Discussion Question 2 as an embedded assessment or as a writing prompt for a science journal entry.)

**3.** Were students able to identify arithmetic and geometric patterns associated with optical illusions? (Use Discussion Question 3 as an embedded assessment or as a writing prompt for a science journal entry.)

**RUBRIC 17.1**
**Sample rubric using these assessment options**

| | Achievement Level | | |
|---|---|---|---|
| | Developing 1 | Proficient 2 | Exemplary 3 |
| Were students able to explain the causes of some optical illusions and variances in visual perception? | Attempted to explain but were unable to do so to any significant extent | Successfully explained causes for these illusions | Successfully explained causes in detail and used appropriate terminology |
| Did students successfully make their own optical illusions for display? | Attempted to make their own illusion but were not successful | Successfully made their own optical illusions | Successfully made their own optical illusions and could explain them in detail |
| Were students able to identify arithmetic and geometric patterns associated with optical illusions? | Attempted to identify patterns but were unable to do so to any significant extent | Successfully identified arithmetic and geometric patterns within the illusions | Successfully identified arithmetic and geometric patterns within the illusions and could describe them in detail using appropriate terminology |

## Going Further

For an art connection, show the class an overhead transparency of Figure 17.8 (the "vase/faces"). Try to see both perspectives at once. Can it be done? Using paints or other media, have students create their own vase/faces figures. Have them try the illusions on each other. Are there two perspectives in each figure?

**FIGURE 17.8. What do you see?**

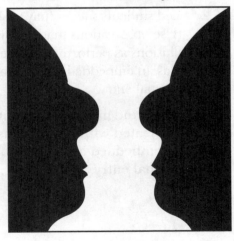

Students can use their vase/faces for a homework survey. Instruct them to conduct a survey of at least 10 people (not students in your class), showing them the vase/faces figure and recording their first impression. Before the survey is conducted, ask students, "Which perspective (vase or faces) do you predict will be more frequently seen first, or will it be even split between vase and faces? Why do you predict that? Which perspective did you see first? Did you predict the same perspective that you saw first? Why or why not?" The next day compare student data, discussing the results and looking for patterns in the responses.

Finally, consider how perspective affects paintings. Show students a variety of representational paintings (e.g., still life, landscape, and/or portrait styles). Ask, "How would the paintings differ if portrayed from a different perspective? What other perspectives were available to the artist? Why do you think that he or she chose this particular perspective?" Students can paint or draw a particular scene (perhaps a still life scene that you set up in class) several times, each time from a different perspective. Ask the class how they feel about the resulting products, how perspective affected the portrayals, and which piece they like best and least and why.

## Other Options and Extensions

1. With the class, investigate stereograms, such as those from Magic Eye books (see *www.magiceye.com*). In a sense, these images are similar to the "old lady/young lady" illustration because a viewer can't see both perspectives simultaneously. Students should research how stereograms are made, and then practice seeing the stereoscopic, three-dimensional images. Are all students able to do so? If not, can they be "taught" to see? What sorts of directions work best for those who had been unable to see the three-dimensional image? Record all observations.

2. With the class, investigate 1960s style *op art* by such artists as Vasarely, Bridget Riley, and Richard Anuszkiewicz. When viewing op art pieces, the eye searches for a comfortable point of focus, and the retina becomes fatigued when it is unable to find one. After-images then occur following retinal fatigue. The repetitive and high-contrast appearance of op art adds to the viewer's perceptual confusion. Students can verbalize and document their visual sensations as they observe pieces of op art. Have students create op art of their own.

## Resources

Churchill, E. R. 1990. *Paper science toys*. New York: Sterling.

Denniston, E. 2002. What a puzzle. *Science and Children* 39 (8): 14–18.

Filliman, P. 1999. Patterns all around. *Teaching Children Mathematics* 5: 390–394.

Marsh, J., J. Loesing, and M. Soucie. 2004. Gee-whiz geometry. *Teaching Children Mathematics* 11 (4): 208–209.

N. E. Thing Enterprises. 1993. *Magic eye: A new way of looking at the world*. Kansas City, MO: Andrews and McMeel.

Thompson, K. B., and D. S. Loftus. 1995. *Art connections: Integrating art throughout the curriculum*. Glenview, IL: Good Year Books.

# +Life Science

## Activity 18

### Determining the Relationship Between Height and Hand Length

## Overview

In this calculation-rich activity, students determine whether a mathematical relationship exists between their personal height and hand length. Designed for older students, this lesson promotes mathematical reasoning, including the use and interpretation of bar and line graphs. The process doesn't become too abstract, however, because all data are based on students' own measurements of their own bodies. The activity integrates applied mathematics with scientific inquiry and the visual arts.

## Processes/Skills

- Observing
- Measuring
- Predicting
- Describing
- Comparing
- Inferring from data
- Designing investigations
- Communicating
- Graphing
- Recognizing mathematical relationships
- Problem solving
- Cooperating
- Creating
- Reflecting

## DETERMINING THE RELATIONSHIP BETWEEN HEIGHT AND HAND LENGTH

## Recommended For

*Grades 6–8: Individual or small-group instruction*
You can adjust this activity for grade 6 by conducting Procedures 6–8, the graphing and analysis, as a whole-class exercise rather than in small groups.

## Time Required

3–4 hours

## Materials Required for Main Activity

- Butcher paper (enough so that each student can make a body outline)
- Crayons/pencils
- Paint or other means of decorating body outline
- Plaster of paris/clay
- Metersticks
- Graph paper

## Connecting to the Standards

### NSES
**Grade 5–8 Content Standards:**
Standard A: Science as Inquiry

- Abilities necessary to do scientific inquiry (especially observing carefully, thinking critically about evidence to develop and communicate good explanations, and using mathematics effectively)

- Understanding about scientific inquiry (especially recognizing the importance of mathematics in science and noticing that scientific explanations emphasize evidence and logically consistent arguments)

Standard C: Life Science

- Structure and function in living systems (especially regarding the structural organization of the human body)

### NCTM
**Standards for Grades 3–8:**

- Numbers and Operations (especially using numbers and operations to solve problems)

- Measurement (especially understanding and applying the metric system)

- Data Analysis and Probability (especially displaying relevant data to answer questions)

- Problem Solving (especially applying strategies to solve a mathematical problem)

- Reasoning and Proof (especially engaging in thinking and reasoning)

- Communication (especially communicating their mathematical thinking clearly)

## Safety Considerations
Basic classroom safety practices apply.

## Activity Objectives
In this activity, students

- measure and document the two variables, height and hand length, by making a body outline and a hand cast; and

- determine the quantitative and graphic relationship between height and hand length and explain their conclusions.

## Background Information
Any investigation of body measurement may bring up challenging, even painful, issues of body image, even with young children. The sensitive teacher will be careful to avoid placing any child "on the spot," especially in front of the child's peers. It is strongly recommended that personal references, direct student-to-student comparisons, and generalizations related to body aesthetics be carefully avoided throughout this activity. An option, of course, would be to skip Procedure 3 altogether and simply measure student heights for Activity Sheet 18.1 and subsequent data analysis.

## Main Activity, Step-by-Step Procedures

**1.** Ask students to look around the classroom and silently notice how our bodies differ. For instance, everyone is a different height. Then ask, "What are some predictors of a person's height? That is, what are some things that, if you knew them about a person, would tell you something about how tall that person is?" Encourage a variety of answers.

**SCIENCE**
Abilities necessary to do
  scientific inquiry

**MATH**
Measurement

**SCIENCE**
Structure and function in
  living systems

**MATH**
Numbers and operations

2.  Ask students to predict how a person's height may be related to the length of his or her hand. Will longer hands belong to taller people, vice versa, or neither? How do students explain their responses? How could we test these hypotheses? Students will probably suggest that we measure and find out for ourselves.

3.  Have students form small groups, and then outline each other's bodies as they lie down on sheets of butcher paper. Arms should rest comfortably at sides and toes should point straight up. The body outlines can then be decorated with paint, crayons, or colored pencils. Better yet, consider decorating the outlines in new ways, for instance, with cut-up bits of colored paper in mosaic fashion, using magazine illustrations and photos to make human collages, or painting with watercolors.

4.  When all the body portraits are completed, have each student measure the head-to-toe length of his or her outline in centimeters and record the length on Activity Sheet 18.1, p. 185. Document everyone's data on the chalkboard. As a class or in small groups, have students compute the range (lowest and highest values), mean (the average), median (the middle measurement in the set of data), and mode (the most frequently occurring value) from the data. Make a bar graph of student heights, using height intervals (for instance, under 70 cm, 71–100 cm, 101–130 cm, 131–160 cm, over 160 cm). Recall the original question about the relationship between height and hand length. Say, "What data do we need now? Hand length, of course!"

5.  To better observe overall hand structure, students make casts of right hands (or left if you prefer, or the individual's dominant hand, as long as all students cast the same thing) in plaster or some similar substance (clay, dough made of flour and water). Hands should be cast flat, a centimeter or two deep, with fingers and thumb pointing directly forward (see Figure 18.1). This is a negative hand cast; a positive cast could also be used for this investigation by making a negative cast in damp sand and filling the "hand" with plaster or wax. If time is limited, simply measure hand length using a pencil-and-paper outline of the hand. After allowing the cast (either negative or positive) to harden, students should begin noting and recording (on Activity Sheet 18.1) observations regarding their hand structures. They should respond to the following questions: Which finger extends farthest? Which is longer, the ring or index finger? How long is each finger, in centimeters? How does the thumb length compare with finger lengths? How long is the entire hand, in centimeters, from the heel to

the tip of the longest finger (see Figure 18.2)? Students should also compare their own hand structures with those of their peers. Ask, "How great is the variation in finger length between individuals? In hand length? How do you know?" Share and discuss findings as a class activity. Record class hand length data on the chalkboard. Compute mean, median, and mode. Have students make bar graphs of class hand lengths, using length intervals (for instance, under 12 cm, 12–14 cm, 14–16 cm, 16–18 cm, over 18 cm).

**FIGURE 18.1. Hand impression**

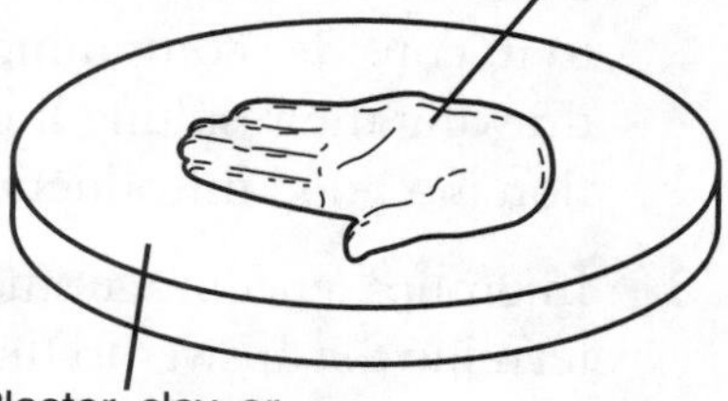

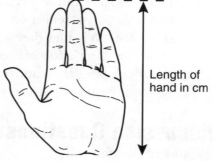

Hand is pressed 1–2 cm deep

Plaster, clay, or dough made of flour and water

**FIGURE 18.2. Hand length**

Length of hand in cm

6. Remind students of the original question in this inquiry: How is height related to hand length? Ask, "Is it easy to see a relationship by just looking at the two lists of data? What could we do to answer our original question? How about a graph? What kind of graph or other portrayal of the data would show us what we want to know?" Consider student responses and their rationale for those responses. Encourage them to reflect on the potential effectiveness of their responses. Let them give it a try, in groups, and see what they come up with. Reflect again.

7. If no one has already done so, suggest generating a coordinate graph of height versus hand length for each student. By looking for a trend (a "line" pointing up, pointing down, lying horizontal, or standing vertical) in the graph's points, this portrayal may show how the variables (i.e., height and hand length) are related. First, students record the heights and associated hand lengths (on Activity Sheet 18.1). Next, each student group graphs the students' data, using height as abscissa (*x* axis) and the associated hand length as ordinate (*y* axis). Now, encourage students to look for a trend in the "cloud" of points on the graph. If the graph is drawn on the chalk-

**MATH**
Problem solving

**MATH**
Data analysis and
  probability

**DETERMINING THE RELATIONSHIP BETWEEN HEIGHT AND HAND LENGTH**

**SCIENCE**
Understanding about
  scientific inquiry

**MATH**
Reasoning and proof
Communication

board or via overhead projector, use a meterstick to find the "best" approximation of the line that "summarizes" the data point cloud, if such a line seems to exist. (If the points are really scattered, no linear approximation may be feasible.) If you and your class are up to it, consider computing the intercept and slope for the data and drawing the resulting line. For very advanced groups, this investigation is a good introduction to studies of correlation and regression.

8.  In groups, encourage students to examine their graphs and to determine the answer to the original query: How is height related to hand length, if it is quantitatively related at all? What responses do they have, and how do they explain their thinking? Do the statistics (mean, median, mode) help? Does the graph help? If so, how? Once the groups have come to their conclusions, individuals may clarify their thoughts and reflections in a journal writing assignment. Be sure to have students reflect on their predictions regarding these measurements. Whether they were "right" or "wrong" they still learned about the association between height and hand length. The value of a working prediction and/or hypothesis is in how it helps us proceed with our inquiry; it directs methods, analysis, and conclusions.

## Discussion Questions

Ask students the following:

1.  How are human bodies similar in terms of their basic structure? How are they different?

2.  According to your data, was height associated with hand length? How do you know? Did one seem to *cause* the other? How do you know?

3.  How did the graphs help you reach your conclusions?

4.  Why do we want to collect as many data points as possible in a study like this? That is, why would it have been difficult to reach a believable conclusion if we had studied only two or three students?

## Assessment

Suggestions for specific ways to assess student understanding are provided in parentheses.

1.  Were students able to document and measure the two variables, height and hand length, by making a body outline and hand cast, respectively? (Use observations made during Procedures 1–5 as performance assessments.)

2. Were students able to determine the quantitative and graphic relationship between height and hand length? Could they explain their conclusions effectively? (Use observations made during Procedures 6–8 as performance assessments, and use Discussion Questions 1–4 as embedded evidence or as writing prompts for science journal entries.)

**RUBRIC 18.1**
**Sample rubric using these assessment options**

| | Achievement Level | | |
| --- | --- | --- | --- |
| | Developing 1 | Proficient 2 | Exemplary 3 |
| Were students able to document and measure the two variables, height and hand length, by making a body outline and hand cast, respectively? | Attempted these activities but without significant success | Successfully completed these activities | Successfully completed these activities and could explain the process in detail |
| Were students able to determine the quantitative and graphic relationship between height and hand length? Could they explain their conclusions effectively? | Attempted to determine these relationships but without significant success | Successfully determined these relationships and offered a basic explanation of their conclusions | Successfully determined these relationships and offered a detailed explanation of their conclusions using appropriate terminology |

# Other Options and Extensions

1. Ask students, "How would adult data of heights and hand lengths compare with the student data you collected and analyzed?" Have students hypothesize (consider hypothesizing not only in words, but graphically, by predicting what the adult height versus hand length "best fit" line would look like), and then test their predictions by collecting data from significant adults in their lives (measuring height and hand length at home with paper metersticks that can be made in class). Make another data table using student-collected data and make another graph. Compare the "best fit" line with that of the student-based graph (from Procedure 7). How accurate were the predictions?

2. Have students think about other species. They could examine the relationship between dogs' body length and hind leg length or between cats' height and tail length. Encourage students to come up with other relationships.

**3.** Have the class compare its height and hand data with data collected from another class. How do the results compare? Did the same mathematical relationship hold for the other class's data?

## Resources

Battista, M. T. 2006. Understanding the development of students' thinking about length. *Teaching Children Mathematics* 13 (3): 140–146.

Beckstead, L. 2008. Scientific journals: A creative assessment. *Science and Children* 46 (3): 22–26.

Cloke, G., N. Ewing, and D. Stevens. 2002. Growing and then sum. *Teaching Children Mathematics* 8 (8): 464.

Kamii, C. 2006. Measurement of length: How can we teach it? *Teaching Children Mathematics* 13 (3): 154–158.

Kubota-Zarivnij, K. 1999. How do you measure a dad? *Teaching Children Mathematics* 6 (4): 260.

Parker, S. 1988. *Eyewitness books: Skeleton*. New York: Knopf.

Phillips, J. 1983. Space age meter. *Science and Children* 21 (2): 9–11.

Ruggles, J., and B. S. Slenger. 1998. The measure me doll. *Teaching Children Mathematics* 5: 40–44.

Slesnick, I. L. 1982. Investigating the human skeleton. *Science and Children* 20 (1): 24, 37–38.

## ACTIVITY SHEET 18.1
## Determining the Relationship Between Height and Hand Length

1. Prediction: Do you think that height is related to hand length? If so, how is it related? What makes you think so?

2. What is your height, head to toe, in cm?  _____ cm

   Class height data:

   Range _____     Mean _____     Median _____     Mode _____

   Make a bar graph of the class height data.

3. How long is your hand, from heel to the tip of the longest finger, in cm?  _____ cm

   Class hand length data:

   Range _____     Mean _____     Median _____     Mode _____

   Make a bar graph of the class hand length data.

4. Make a coordinate graph of height (*x* axis) versus hand length (*y* axis), using data from the table below. Enter class data for each student:

| Student Height | Student Hand Length |
|---|---|
|  |  |
|  |  |
|  |  |
|  |  |
|  |  |
|  |  |
|  |  |
|  |  |
|  |  |
|  |  |
|  |  |
|  |  |
|  |  |
|  |  |

5. Based on your analysis of the data, is student height related to hand length? If so, how? How do you know?

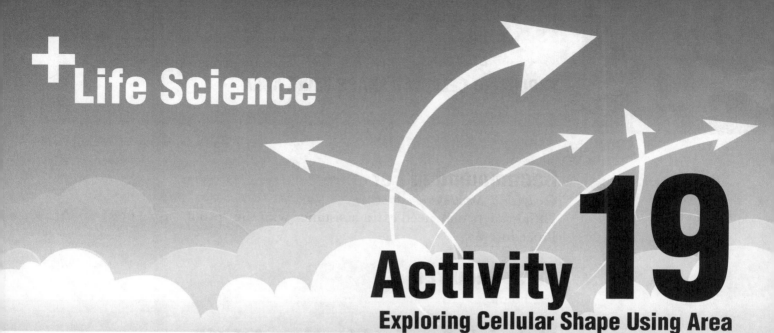

## Overview

In this activity, students are challenged to maximize the area enclosed within the limited perimeter of a string "cell membrane," using area formulas as they do so. This is an open-ended activity that will challenge groups of students to apply mathematical thinking to a problem in cell biology. They will confront the issue of cellular shape and the differences between area and volume in a practical setting.

## Processes/Skills

- Observing
- Measuring
- Communicating
- Developing spatial and geometric reasoning
- Comparing
- Reflecting
- Recognizing shapes and patterns
- Problem solving
- Analyzing
- Designing
- Applying area formulas
- Communicating
- Cooperating

## Recommended For

*Grades 5–8: Small-group instruction*

Fifth graders may need extra assistance with the "proof" aspect of Procedure 2.

## Time Required

1–2 hours

## Materials Required for Main Activity

- String
- Metric rulers
- Calculators

## Connecting to the Standards

### NSES
**Grade 5–8 Content Standards:**

Standard A: Science as Inquiry

- Abilities necessary to do scientific inquiry (especially thinking critically about evidence to develop and communicate good explanations, and using mathematics effectively)

- Understanding about scientific inquiry (especially recognizing the importance of mathematics in science)

Standard C: Life Science

- Structure and function in living systems (especially regarding the general structure of cells)

- Diversity and adaptations of organisms (especially regarding biological adaptations that enhance species survival)

### NCTM
**Standards for Grades 3–8:**

- Numbers and Operations (especially using numbers and operations to solve problems)

- Geometry (especially identifying, naming, and comparing two-dimensional shapes)

- Measurement (especially understanding and applying the metric system)
- Problem Solving (especially applying strategies to solve problems)
- Reasoning and Proof (especially engaging in thinking and reasoning)

## Safety Considerations
Basic classroom safety practices apply.

## Activity Objectives
In this activity, students

- use area formulas of circle, square, rectangle, and triangle to maximize the surface area of a cell; and
- understand why cells tend to be round.

## Main Activity, Step-by-Step Procedures

1. Explain that all living things are made of cells (this concept is known as the *cell theory*). Check for students' background understanding of cells by asking them to draw some cells and to describe their shapes to the class. Explain that cells usually need maximum surface area for transfer and exchange of materials across the *cell membrane* (the outer surface of the cell). Given a certain amount of surface area for a particular, single cell, what general shape must the cell be to maximize its volume? This is a particularly important point for cells that store materials, such as fat cells. The answer to the question lies in the cell's general shape. Students will solve this problem, though, in two dimensions rather than three for the sake of simplicity (that is, working with two-dimensional *area* rather than in three-dimensional *volume*).

2. In this activity, students should work in groups of three or four. Each group receives a 1 m length of string, a meterstick, and a calculator. The string represents the cell membrane (in two dimensions) of a cell students are going to "build." The challenge: Each group must make as large a cell as possible with the string, using any of four basic geometric shapes (circle, square, rectangle, or triangle). Students may solve the problem any way that they like, but they must be able to prove that their shape solution is largest using the formulas for area ($\pi r^2$, length × width, or ½ length × width). (The circle encloses the largest area for any given perimeter, as student calculations should show.)

### SCIENCE
Abilities necessary to do scientific inquiry
Structure and function in living systems
Diversity and adaptations of organisms

### MATH
Problem solving

### MATH
Numbers and operations
Geometry
Measurement

### SCIENCE
Understanding about scientific inquiry

### MATH
Reasoning and proof

3.  When all groups have completed the task, have each group of students report their approach to solving the problem, their solution, and their computational evidence. The ensuing discussion may become lively, particularly if some students disagree about the round shape being best. Be sure to base the evidence in area formulas and calculations. Encourage students to reflect on their methods, their grasp of the area formulas, and their calculations.

## Discussion Questions

Ask students the following:

1.  Would you be surprised to find that many cells are round or oval shaped? Explain your answer.

2.  How are area formulas useful? Can you think of some ways that they might be useful to you or to people you know?

3.  How do real cells differ from the one you "made" with your string membrane?

## Assessment

Suggestions for specific ways to assess student understanding are provided in parentheses.

1.  Were students able to use the area formulas to either solve the problem or serve as evidence of their decision? (Use observations made during Procedure 2 as performance assessments, and use Discussion Question 2 as embedded evidence or as a writing prompt for a science journal entry.)

2.  Could students explain why many cells tend to be round in shape? (Use Discussion Questions 1 and 3 as embedded assessments or as writing prompts for science journal entries.)

**RUBRIC 19.1**
**Sample rubric using these assessment options**

| | Achievement Level | | |
| --- | --- | --- | --- |
| | Developing 1 | Proficient 2 | Exemplary 3 |
| Were students able to use the area formulas to either solve the problem or serve as evidence of their decision? | Attempted but were not successful to any significant extent | Successfully used area formulas to solve the problem and/or to serve as evidence of their decision | Successfully used area formulas to solve the problem and to serve as evidence of their decision, and were able to explain in detail, using appropriate terminology |
| Could students explain why many cells tend to be round in shape? | Attempted to explain but were not successful to any significant extent | Successfully explained why many cells tend to be round in shape | Successfully explained why many cells tend to be round in shape, and did so in detail, using appropriate terminology |

# Options and Extensions

1. Remind students that not all cells are round or oval. Ask, "Can you discover some cells that have other shapes? Are their shapes related to their functions, and if so, how?" (Consider epithelial cells, neurons, or red blood cells.)

2. Have students look at different types of cells under a microscope. You can use prepared slides or have students make their own slides using pond life or other samples from the local environment.

3. Ask students, "If you wanted to make a chicken coop and you had only 10 yd. of chicken wire to use, what shape would make the coop as big as possible?" Have students explain their answers.

## Resources

Cantlon, D. 1998. Kids + conjecture + mathematics power. *Teaching Children Mathematics* 5: 108–112.

Hopkins, M. 1996. Picket fences. *Teaching Children Mathematics* 3: 86–90.

Nitabach, E., and R. Lehrer. 1996. Developing spatial sense through area measurement. *Teaching Children Mathematics* 2: 473–476.

Way, V. 1982. Sculpting cells with Play Doh. *Science and Children* 20 (2): 25.

Yang, D. 2006. Developing number sense through real-life situations. *Teaching Children Mathematics* 13 (2): 104–106.

# Activity 20

## Please Pass the Pollen: Flowering Plants, Pollination, and Insect Pollinators

## Overview

This high-interest activity provides an opportunity for students to learn more about the natural world while they hone their investigatory skills. In the activity, student groups investigate pollination, insect behavior, and flower structure. They will design and carry out experiments of their choosing as they apply the inquiry skills learned in other activities in this book. In a Going Further activity, students design and "build" an artificial flower that will attract pollinators.

## Processes/Skills

- Observing
- Counting
- Predicting
- Describing
- Inferring
- Recognizing mathematical relationships
- Experimenting
- Communicating
- Reflecting
- Recognizing patterns
- Problem solving
- Creating
- Cooperating

**PLEASE PASS THE POLLEN: FLOWERING PLANTS, POLLINATION, AND INSECT POLLINATORS**

## Recommended For

*Grades 6–8: Small-group or whole-class instruction*
You can adapt this activity for sixth graders by choosing a particular pollination question or questions for students to investigate, and even pursue the inquiry as a whole class.

## Time Required

2–4 hours

## Materials Required for Main Activity

- Flowering plants (Use plants already on the school grounds and/or potted plants—check with a local nursery or the internet to determine the most pollinator-friendly plants for your bio-region.)
- Hand lenses (and/or dissecting or compound microscopes if available)
- Calculators

## Materials Required for Going Further

- A variety of materials for creating artificial flowers (including various types of paper, inks, paints, pens, tape, glue, and fragrances)
- Wire
- Bamboo plant supports, bamboo skewers, or pipe cleaners to serve as artificial flower "stems"

## Connecting to the Standards

### NSES
**Grade 5–8 Content Standards:**
Standard A: Science as Inquiry

- Abilities necessary to do scientific inquiry (especially observing carefully, thinking critically about evidence to develop and communicate good explanations, and using mathematics effectively)
- Understanding about scientific inquiry (especially recognizing the importance of mathematics in science and noticing that scientific explanations emphasize evidence and logically consistent arguments)

Standard C: Life Science

- Structure and function in living systems (especially regarding the structure and function of pollinators and their plants)

- Regulation and behavior (especially investigating pollination-related regulation and behavior)

- Diversity and adaptations of organisms (especially regarding biological adaptations that enhance species survival)

### NCTM
#### Standards for Grades 3–8:

- Data Analysis and Probability (especially displaying relevant data to answer questions)

- Problem Solving (especially applying strategies to solve problems)

- Reasoning and Proof (especially engaging in thinking and reasoning)

- Connections (especially recognizing the connections among mathematical ideas and to investigations outside mathematics)

## Safety Considerations

Basic classroom safety practices apply. In addition, inform students ahead of time that they must not disturb the pollinators—especially those that are members of order Hymenoptera, i.e., bees and wasps—by keeping calm and remaining at a respectful distance (at least a meter away). Identify students with pollen allergies and/or sensitivity to insect stings ahead of time and be sure to keep them far out of harm's way. If there are significant concerns about stinging pollinators, focus on plants pollinated heavily by the nonstinging order Lepidoptera, that is, by butterflies and moths (for instance, butterfly bush, nasturtium, poppy, aster, and lavender).

## Activity Objectives

In this activity, students

- design experiments to test their ideas and predictions about pollination;

- reach accurate and thoughtful conclusions regarding pollination based on their observations; and

- apply mathematical thinking to their pollination investigations.

**PLEASE PASS THE POLLEN: FLOWERING PLANTS, POLLINATION, AND INSECT POLLINATORS**

## Background Information

This activity differs somewhat from others in this book because a great deal of the investigation occurs outside the classroom, and because it requires some special materials, i.e., a fairly large number of living, flowering plants (either plants that you find on campus or those that you and/or the class plant yourselves). It could be undertaken on a smaller scale using several potted plants, however. In any case, you'll want to check ahead to be sure that you have a sufficient number of pollinators visiting whatever flowers you have available. Weather will also affect the number of pollinators visiting your flowers and, as happens so often in scientific investigation, you'll have to adjust and adapt your plans accordingly.

Pollen grains are the dustlike particles produced by the male reproductive organ, the anther, of flowering plants (i.e., angiosperms). Pollination is the deposition of pollen grains on the stigma of the flower's female reproductive organ (see Figure 20.1). Some flowering plants are self-pollinated and others are cross-pollinated, that is, pollen is transferred from the anther of one flower to the stigma of another. Cross-pollination is usually accomplished by wind or by insects (often moths, bees, and butterflies). Once pollination occurs, the pollen grains release sperm cells that fertilize eggs, which develop into seeds.

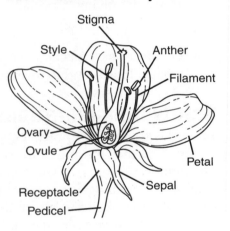

**FIGURE 20.1.**
**Basic flower anatomy**

## Main Activity, Step-by-Step Procedures

1. Begin by asking students to name foods they eat that come from plants. List their responses on the board; the list will most likely be long. Point out that many of those plants would not grow if it weren't for pollinators, which spread the plants' pollen from flower to flower and allow the plants to reproduce and grow fruits and vegetables. We therefore rely on pollinators for much of our food, and many flowering plants rely on pollinators for their very survival. Ask the students what they know about pollinators and pollination.

   Take the class outside to observe some flowers on campus (these can be in the ground or in pots, but the more the better). Have students record their observations of any pollination activity they can see:

**SCIENCE**
Abilities necessary to do scientific inquiry
Regulation and behavior

what sorts of pollinators, which flowers are most often visited, etc. Return to the classroom and have students report their findings. Ask, "What do you want to know about flowers, pollen, and pollinators? How can we investigate and find answers to your questions?" Be sure to adjust the following procedures to students' own notions of experimentation in order to offer opportunities for them to understand effective experimental technique through trial and error.

2. Devise investigations to encourage students to find out more about their questions regarding pollination and pollinators by direct observation. This process will be much more valuable if you allow the student groups to devise their own investigations, scaffolded by your comments and suggestions. They will practice determining the empirical means to answer their own questions.

   For instance,

   - How often are flowers visited by pollinators? (Students can predict and count the number of pollinators visiting a particular flower or a particular area of flowers within a certain time, such as 10 minutes. Then they can determine how many pollinators would be expected to visit that flower or area in an hour or a day.)

   - Is pollination more likely to occur in morning or afternoon? (Students can make observations at different times of the day and compare their results.)

   - Are different pollinators active at different times of the day (e.g., morning versus afternoon)? (Again, observations made throughout the day may be compared to provide insight.)

   - Do different flowers attract different pollinators? Does flower color seem to have anything to do with pollinator type or number of visits? (Compare data to find out.)

3. Bring some flowers, both large and small, into the classroom for observation with hand lenses, microscopes, and/or dissecting scopes. Students can carefully dissect the flowers under a lens and watch for small or hidden insects. Are there any insect pollinators present that you might have missed seeing in the field?

   Clearly, students have unlimited opportunities to use math to analyze pollinator behavior: How long does a butterfly remain on a particular flower? What does it do while it's on the flower? Does it move on to a nearby flower or fly away, and approximately how far does it

**SCIENCE**
Structure and function in
   living systems
Diversity and adaptations
   of organisms

**MATH**
Problem solving

**SCIENCE**
Understanding about
   scientific inquiry

**MATH**
Data analysis and
   probability
Reasoning and proof
Connections

move? How many flowers does it visit before leaving the area? Within a given time on a particular flower, how many insects are present? (Consider comparing the *mean*, i.e., the average, with the *mode*, i.e., the most frequently occurring number, of insects on a particular flower.) Data can also be used to create bar graphs, such as three bars comparing the number of insects seen on three different types of flowers. Students should see that by combining individual data, they have more evidence on which to base their conclusions. They should also be encouraged to reflect on their methodologies, before and after carrying out their investigations. For instance, ask students, "Do you foresee any problems with this experimental technique? What were some sources of error in your investigations? How would you proceed differently if you were to do the investigations again?"

## Discussion Questions

Ask students the following:

1. For what foods do we depend on pollinators? In what other ways do pollinators affect our lives?

2. Pollination can be thought of like an "arranged deal" between the flower and the pollinator, with both parties benefiting from the relationship. How does the flower benefit? How does the pollinator benefit? Who or what else benefits? (In scientific jargon, we might call the relationship in which both parties benefit a *mutualistic* instance of *symbiosis*.)

3. How are flowers adapted for insect pollination? How are the insect pollinators adapted for pollinating flowers?

4. How did you use mathematics in your studies of pollination? How would your pollination experiments or investigations have been different if you had not used math?

5. How would our lives be different without insect pollinators? What can we do to ensure that insect pollinators survive and thrive?

## Assessment

Suggestions for specific ways to assess student understanding are provided in parentheses.

1. Were students able to effectively design experiments to test their ideas and predictions about pollination? (Use the outcomes of Procedure 2 as a performance assessment.)

2.  Did students reach accurate and thoughtful conclusions regarding pollination based on their observations? (Use Discussion Questions 1–5 as embedded assessments or as prompts for writing science journal entries.)

3.  Were students able to successfully apply mathematics to their investigations of pollinators and pollination? (Use Discussion Question 4 as an embedded assessment or as a prompt for writing a science journal entry.)

## RUBRIC 20.1
### Sample rubric using these assessment options

| | Achievement Level | | |
|---|---|---|---|
| | **Developing**<br>**1** | **Proficient**<br>**2** | **Exemplary**<br>**3** |
| Were students able to effectively design experiments to test their ideas and predictions about pollination? | Attempted to design an experiment but were unsuccessful to any significant extent | Successfully designed and carried out a pollination-related experiment | Successfully designed and carried out a pollination-related experiment and were able to explain their investigation in detail using appropriate terminology |
| Did students reach accurate and thoughtful conclusions regarding pollination based on their observations? | Attempted to reach thoughtful conclusions but were unable to do so to any significant extent | Successfully reached accurate and thoughtful conclusions based on their observations | Successfully reached accurate and thoughtful conclusions based on their observations and were able to explain their work in detail using appropriate terminology |
| Were students able to successfully apply mathematics to their investigations of pollinators and pollination? | Attempted to apply math to their inquiry but were unsuccessful to any significant extent | Successfully applied math to their pollination inquiry | Successfully applied math to their pollination inquiry and were able to explain their work in detail using appropriate terminology |

# Going Further

Begin this art connection by asking, "What sorts of flowers seem to attract insect pollinators? What are the characteristics of an insect-attractive flower?" Consider primary attractants (e.g., nectar and pollen availability, that is, nutrition) and secondary attractants (e.g., color, odor, shape, temperature, motion, placement/location). Direct the student groups to design and build a flower that will attract as many insects as possible or that will attract a particular type of insect. (Most flowers are at least somewhat specific about attracting only a few types of pollinators, whereas some are linked to a single species of insect.) Offer a variety of materials for flower building, including various types of paper, inks, paints, pens, tape, glue, and fragrances. Wire, bamboo plant supports, bamboo skewers, or pipe cleaners will work well as flower stems. Or you could simplify the process by providing artificial flowers that the students can embellish with paint, fragrance, etc. Ask the students to predict the types of insects that will be attracted to their flower. Take the completed flowers outside and "plant" them. Have students record the type and number of pollinators that visit within a certain time period. On average, how long did insects remain on these artificial flowers? Return to the classroom and discuss the data. Have students explore the following questions: What conclusions can be reached? What sorts of attractants were effective? Which were ineffective? How did "time on artificial flower" compare with "time on real flower"? What surprised you about this investigation? What else do you want to know about this topic?

## Other Options and Extensions

1. Options and extensions here are nearly limitless. Students could find out more about angiosperms, flower structure, pollen structure and function, or the life cycles of the insect pollinators. They might also be interested in researching coevolution (that is, the joint evolution of two or more different species in which selection pressure operates to make the evolution of either species partially dependent on the evolution of the other) of flowers and their pollinators (consider the passion flower and the *Heliaconius* butterfly, the yucca flower and the yucca moth, or the hummingbird and the chuparosa [*Beloperone californica*] or *Penstemon* flowers). Other topics of interest might include carnivorous plants, bees and beekeeping, the significant loss of bee pollinators in North America, and the dispersal of "killer bees" (Africanized bees) into the United States from Central and South America.

2. Students can do more in-depth studies of flower anatomy, which might include pressing various flowers (in a plant press, see Figure 20.2, or between pieces of newsprint placed between the pages of a heavy book). Pressed flowers make beautiful and useful displays when glued onto paper.

## FIGURE 20.2. Plant press

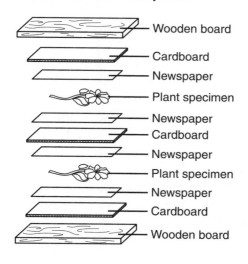

Wooden board
Cardboard
Newspaper
Plant specimen
Newspaper
Cardboard
Newspaper
Plant specimen
Newspaper
Cardboard
Wooden board

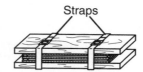

Straps

You can stack many plant specimens in a single press, which is cinched tightly together with straps. Remove specimens when completely dry.

For each specimen, collect part of the stem and foliage along with the flower, keeping all parts intact and connected. Record collection location, date, specimen name, and pollinators observed on the flowers.

## Resources

Dobey, D. C., and H. S. Springer. 2002. Simply butterflies. *Science and Children* 40 (3): 16–21.

Faegri, K., and L. van der Pijl. 1979. *The principles of pollination ecology.* 3rd ed. New York: Pergamon Press.

Forrest, K., D. Schnabel, and M. E. Williams. 2006. A-buzz about math. *Teaching Children Mathematics* 13 (2): 96–97.

Heinrich, B. 2004. *Bumblebee economics.* Cambridge, MA: Harvard University Press.

Hinman, L. A. 2000. What's the buzz? *Science and Children* 37 (5): 24–27.

Moore, G. J. 1991. Flowering in Fairbanks. *Science and Children* 29 (3): 29–30.

Pianka, E. R. 1983. *Evolutionary ecology.* 3rd ed. New York: Harper and Row.

Radue, A. K. 1991. The amaryllis—From bulb to blossom. *Science and Children* 29 (3): 27–28.

Scribner-MacLean, M., and K. McLaughlin. 2005. The human side of butterflies. *Science and Children* 43 (2): 24–27.

Seidel, J. D. 1998. Symmetry in season. *Teaching Children Mathematics* 4: 244–249.

# Interdisciplinary Resources

## Science and Mathematics
### Specific Ideas for Lesson Development

Goldston, M. J., ed. 2004. *Stepping up to science and math: Exploring the natural connections*. Arlington, VA: NSTA Press.

*Great Explorations in Math and Science* (GEMS)

Kellough, R. D., J. S. Cangelosi, A. T. Collette, E. L. Chiappetta, R. J. Souviney, L. W. Trowbridge, and R. W. Bybee. 1996. *Integrating mathematics and science for intermediate and middle school students*. Englewood Cliffs, NJ: Merrill.

Lawlor, R. 1982. *Sacred geometry: Philosophy and practice*. London: Thames and Hudson.

National Science Teachers Association. 2003. *Mixing it up: Integrated, interdisciplinary, intriguing science in the elementary classroom*. Arlington, VA: NSTA Press.

Project AIMS (Activities Integrating Math and Science)

## Science (or Math) and Art
### Ideas for Lessons and Interdisciplinary Instruction

Churchill, E. R. 1990. *Paper science toys*. New York: Sterling.

Dubeck, L. W., S. E. Moshier, and J. E. Boss. 1988. Science in cinema: *Teaching science fact through science fiction films*. New York: Teachers College Press.

Kohl, M. A., and J. Potter. 1993. *Science arts: Discovering science through art experiences*. Bellingham, WA: Bright Ring.

Nurosi, A. 2000. *Colorful illusions: Tricks to fool your eyes*. New York: Sterling.

Williams, D. 1995. *Teaching mathematics through children's art*. Portsmouth, NH: Heinemann.

## Science Process Activities
### Ideas for Lessons and Interdisciplinary Instruction

Cobb, V. 1979. *More science experiments you can eat*. New York: Harper and Row.

Ingram, M. 1993. *Bottle biology: An idea book for exploring the world through plastic bottles and other recyclable materials*. Dubuque, IA: Kendall/Hunt.

Mandell, M. 1959. *Physics experiments for children.* New York: Dover.

Ostlund, K. L. 1992. *Science process skills: Assessing hands-on student performance.* Menlo Park, CA: Addison-Wesley.

Packard, M. 2006. *Mythbusters: Don't try this at home.* San Francisco: Jossey-Bass.

Rezba, R. J., C. Sprague, R. L. Fiel, and H. J. Funk. 1995. *Learning and assessing science process skills.* 3rd ed. Dubuque, IA: Kendall/Hunt.

Strongin, H. 1991. *Science on a shoestring.* 2nd ed. Menlo Park, CA: Addison-Wesley.

Tolman, M. N., and J. O. Morton. 1986. *Earth science activities for grades 2–8.* West Nyack, NY: Parker.

United Nations Educational, Scientific and Cultural Organization. 1962. *700 science experiments for everyone.* New York: Doubleday.

VanCleave, J. 1989. *Chemistry for every kid: 101 easy experiments that really work.* New York: Wiley.

Walpole, B. 1988. *175 science experiments to amuse and amaze your friends.* New York: Random House.

## Art Ideas and Activities
### Ideas for Lessons and Interdisciplinary Instruction

Cornett, C. E. 1999. *The arts as meaning makers: Integrating literature and the arts throughout the curriculum.* Upper Saddle River, NJ: Merrill.

Goldberg, M. 1997. *Arts and learning: An integrated approach to teaching and learning in multicultural and multilingual settings.* New York: Longman.

Jenkins, P. D. 1980. *Art for the fun of it: A guide for teaching young children.* New York: Fireside.

Olshansky, B. 1990. *Portfolio of illustrated step-by-step art projects for young children.* New York: Center for Applied Research in Education.

Stribling, M. L. 1970. *Art from found materials, discarded and natural.* New York: Crown.

Terzian, A. M. 1993. *The kids' multicultural art book.* Charlotte, VT: Williamson.

Thompson, K. B., and D. S. Loftus. 1995. *Art connections: Integrating art throughout the curriculum (grades 4–8).* Glenview, IL: Good Year Books.

## Science and Science Teaching Information
### Useful Background Information

Craig, A., and C. Rosney. 1988. *The Usborne science encyclopedia.* Tulsa, OK: EDC.

Ebeneezer, J. V., and E. Lau. 1999. *Science on the internet: A resource for K–12 teachers.* Upper Saddle River, NJ: Merrill.

Gabel, D. L. ed. 1994. *Handbook of research on science teaching and learning.* New York: Macmillan.

Kwan, T., and J. Texley. 2002. *Exploring safely: A guide for elementary teachers.* Arlington, VA: NSTA Press.

National Science Teachers Association. 2003. *Safety in the elementary science classroom.* Arlington, VA: NSTA Press.

Roy, K. R. 2007. *The NSTA ready-reference guide to safer science.* Arlington, VA: NSTA Press.

Tobin, K. ed. 1993. *The practice of constructivism in science education.* Washington: AAAS Press.

Trefil, J. 1992. *1001 things everyone should know about science.* New York: Doubleday.

## Professional Journals

*Science and Children*
*Science Scope*
*Teaching Children Mathematics* (formerly *The Arithmetic Teacher*)
*School Science and Mathematics*

## National Standards

American Association for the Advancement of Science. 1993. *Benchmarks for science literacy.* New York: Oxford University Press.

National Council of Teachers of Mathematics. 2000. *Principles and standards for school mathematics.* Reston, VA: Author.

National Council of Teachers of Mathematics. 2006. *Curriculum focal points for prekindergarten through grade 8 mathematics.* Reston, VA: Author.

National Research Council. 1996. *National science education standards.* Washington, DC: National Academy Press.

# Internet Resources

**Chem 4 Kids:** *http://chem4kids.com*
Lessons and background information in chemistry

**Dragonfly:** *www.units.muohio.edu/dragonfly*
Student-friendly, interactive website, including many interdisciplinary lesson ideas for teachers

**The Educator's Reference Desk:** *http://ericir.syr.edu/cgi-bin/printlessons.cgi/Virtual/Lessons/Science/SCI0025.html*
Science lesson ideas, background information, and other resources for teachers

**The Geometry in Space Project:** *www.math-ed.com/Resources/GIS/Geometry_In_Space*
Interactive site with interdisciplinary lesson ideas related to space travel

**Houghton Mifflin Harcourt Education Place Activity Search:** *http://eduplace.com/activity*
Specific lesson ideas in science, math, and other disciplines

**Keep America Beautiful:** *www.kab.org/site/PageServer?pagename=index*
Background information and lesson ideas on recycling and waste reduction

**Kids as Global Scientists:** *www.biokids.umich.edu/research/kgs*
Interdisciplinary lesson ideas, background information, and other resources for teachers and students

**National Council of Teachers of Mathematics:** *www.nctm.org*
All aspects of K–12 classroom math

**National Science Teachers Association:** *www.nsta.org*
All aspects of K–12 classroom science

## INTERNET RESOURCES

**Northwest Regional Educational Laboratory (NWREL) Library in the Sky:** *http://nwrel.org/sky/index.php*
Interdisciplinary lesson ideas

**Science NetLinks:** *http://sciencenetlinks.com*
American Association for the Advancement of Science website; lessons, background information, and other resources

**Thinking Fountain:** *www.thinkingfountain.org*
Many science lesson ideas, including interdisciplinary lessons

**United Nations Cyberschoolbus:** *http://un.org/Pubs/CyberSchoolBus*
United Nations site for human rights/social justice education; interdisciplinary lessons and background information

**The Why Files:** *http://whyfiles.org*
Science, math, and technology news and background information

**Year Long Project:** *http://www.ed.uiuc.edu/ylp*
Many science lesson ideas, including interdisciplinary lessons

# Index

*Page numbers in **boldface** type refer to figures or tables.*

# INDEX

# INDEX

# INDEX

# INDEX

## INDEX

# INDEX

# INDEX